Layman's Bible Book Commentary
2 Corinthians, Galatians, Ephesians

LAYMAN'S BIBLE BOOK COMMENTARY

LBBC

2 CORINTHIANS, GALATIANS, EPHESIANS

VOLUME 21

David C. George

BROADMAN PRESS
Nashville, Tennessee

© Copyright 1979 • Broadman Press.

4211-91

ISBN: 0-8054-1191-7

Dewey Decimal Classification: 227

Subject heading: BIBLE.   N.   T.   EPISTLES

Library of Congress Catalog Card Number: 78-74202

Printed in the United States of America

Foreword

The *Layman's Bible Book Commentary* in twenty-four volumes was planned as a practical exposition of the whole Bible for lay readers and students. It is based on the conviction that the Bible speaks to every generation of believers but needs occasional reinterpretation in the light of changing language and modern experience. Following the guidance of God's Spirit, the believer finds in it the authoritative word for faith and life.

To meet the needs of lay readers, the *Commentary* is written in a popular style, and each Bible book is clearly outlined to reveal its major emphases. Although the writers are competent scholars and reverent interpreters, they have avoided critical problems and the use of original languages except where they were essential for explaining the text. They recognize the variety of literary forms in the Bible, but they have not followed documentary trails or become preoccupied with literary concerns. Their primary purpose was to show what each Bible book meant for its time and what it says to our own generation.

The Revised Standard Version of the Bible is the basic text of the *Commentary*, but writers were free to use other translations to clarify an occasional passage or sharpen its effect. To provide as much interpretation as possible in such concise books, the Bible text was not printed along with the comment.

Of the twenty-four volumes of the *Commentary*, fourteen deal with Old Testament books and ten with those in the New Testament. The volumes range in pages from 140 to 168. Four major books in the Old Testament and five in the New are treated in one volume each. Others appear in various combinations. Although the allotted space varies, each Bible book is treated as a whole to reveal its basic message with some passages getting special attention. Whatever plan of Bible study the reader may follow, this *Commentary* will be a valuable companion.

Despite the best-seller reputation of the Bible, the average survey of Bible knowledge reveals a good deal of ignorance about it and its primary meaning. Many adult church members seem to think that its study is intended for children and preachers. But some of the newer translations have been making the Bible more readable for all ages. Bible study has branched out from Sunday into other days of the week, and into neighborhoods rather than just in churches. This *Commentary* wants to meet the growing need for insight into all that the Bible has to say about God and his world and about Christ and his fellowship.

BROADMAN PRESS

Contents

2 CORINTHIANS

GALATIANS

EPHESIANS

The Life and Ministry of Paul

Major Events	Biblical Records		Possible Dates
	Acts	Galatians	
Birth			A.D. 1
Conversion	9:1–25	1:11–17	33
First Jerusalem visit	9:26–30	1:18–20	36
Famine	11:25–30	2:1–10?	46
First missionary journey	13:1 to 14:28		47–48
Apostolic council in Jerusalem	15:1–29	2:1–10?	49
Second missionary journey	15:36 to 18:21		50–53
Letter to the Galatians			53–55
Third missionary journey	18:23 to 21:6		53–57
Letters to the Corinthians			55
Arrest and prison in Jerusalem and Caesarea	21:8 to 26:32		57
Prison in Rome	27:1 to 28:30		60–62
Letter to the Ephesians			60–62
Death			67

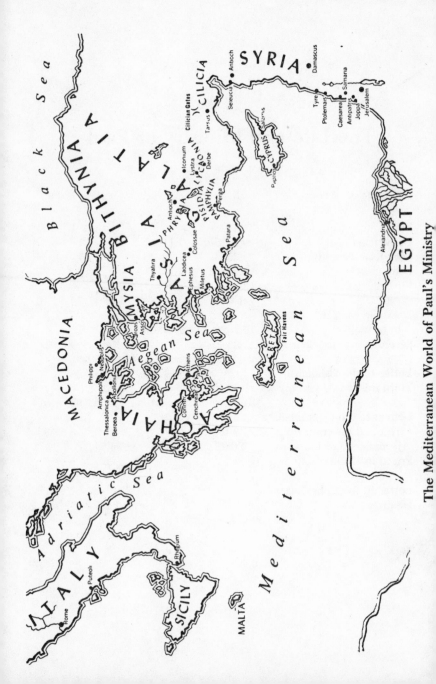

The Mediterranean World of Paul's Ministry

2 CORINTHIANS

Introduction

Paul's second letter to Corinth is third in length among his writings, after Romans and 1 Corinthians. It contains some of his most profound theology. In it he shared more about himself and his feelings than he did anywhere else. And yet this book is probably less read and understood than any of his other letters. Why is this? The mystery of the neglected masterpiece can only be solved by a careful look at the background and content of the book.

Background

Corinth was the leading business center in ancient Greece. It stood on the narrow strip of land joining northern and southern Greece. Merchandise arrived at Cenchreae on the east or Lechaeum on the west and was carried overland to the other side. In this way ships could follow a more northerly route and avoid the storms which occurred farther out in the Mediterranean Sea. An international city, Corinth was subject to many intellectual and religious influences. The goddess Aphrodite was worshiped there in a great temple served by a thousand priestesses who were also religious prostitutes.

Paul first came to Corinth around A.D. 50 (Acts 18:1). He was on his second missionary journey and had launched a tour of Greece beginning in the northeastern territory of Macedonia. He stayed in Corinth for a year and one-half (Acts 18:11) before returning to Antioch in Syria to close the second journey. He soon came back to Ephesus, where he continued to give attention to the work at Corinth.

Developments at Corinth are not clear, but scholars have pieced together a likely description of what happened. Apollos had remained at Corinth to carry on the work (Acts 18:27-28; 19:1). Soon he came to Ephesus bringing reports of serious problems in Corinth. Paul wrote a letter which is not preserved in the New Testament, warning against immorality (1 Cor. 5:9).

Another report, brought by members of Chloe's family, told Paul

that there were quarrels going on in the church (1 Cor. 1:11). Paul
dispatched Timothy to deal with the problem (1 Cor. 4:17). Meanwhile,
a letter arrived from Corinth; and Paul responded by writing 1 Corinthians, around Easter, A.D. 55. The Corinthians began to question
Paul's authority. If Timothy did arrive at Corinth he may have found
this situation impossible to deal with and returned to report to Paul.
We do have evidence that Paul then made a second visit to Corinth
(2 Cor. 2:1; 12:14; 13:1; 2:5-8; 7:12). It is likely that he was received
rudely and that this is the offense he writes about in 2 Corinthians.

After this visit, Paul wrote a stern letter to Corinth (2 Cor. 2:3,9;
7:8-12), probably 2 Corinthians 10—13, which he sent by Titus. Titus
was instructed to return and report to Paul. Paul left Ephesus and
went to Troas to meet Titus and to preach in the area. In his impatience he left Troas and went on to Macedonia to find Titus (2 Cor.
2:12-13). When he found Titus, the report from Corinth was good
(2 Cor. 7:6-16). Paul wrote 2 Corinthians at this point (the fall of
55)—at least the thankful part in chapters 1—9. Titus and two helpers
delivered the letter (2 Cor. 8:16-24). Later Paul visited Corinth a
third time, probably writing the letter to the Romans while there
(Acts 19:21; 20:3).

Content

Second Corinthians is hard to understand. Its main points are clear
enough, but the original Greek is difficult. Then, too, the ideas are
packed so tightly in places that it's hard to see all the meaning. Paul
often refers to ideas and events familiar to his readers but unfamiliar
to us today. All of the letters in the New Testament present this
problem. Their focus on specific problems now unknown to us makes
them lively and practical, but it also makes them hard to interpret.
The problem is intensified in 2 Corinthians by the emotion of the
writer and the complexity of the events.

The letter is difficult to outline. Paul's thoughts pour forth with
great feeling. Scene changes and flashbacks occur almost as in a modern movie. Mention of a fact will often lead to an outburst of praise.
Chapters 8—9 are a distinct unit, but it is not clear that chapters
10—13 are in their original order. Some of the difficulty of the book
comes from the tension under which Paul was writing. His normal
style was to speak of Christ, not himself (4:5). The challenge of his
critics forced him to write about his credentials as an apostle. This

he regarded as a foolish but necessary gesture.

Basically, the book describes and defends the ministry of a great Christian leader. It consists of three major sections. Chapters 1—7 describe Christian ministry as practiced by Paul. Chapters 8—9 tell about a special offering Paul was taking to help needy Christians. Chapters 10—13 defend Paul's ministry against his critics.

It is clear that this writing was brought about by problems between Paul and the Corinthian church. What is not clear is the nature of those problems. We know about immorality and disunity at Corinth from 1 Corinthians, but these don't seem to be in question in the second letter. If we take our clue from what Paul actually says in 2 Corinthians, the problem must be criticism of the apostle by someone in the church. These critics may have been Jewish Christians who recommended themselves as apostles (12:11). The likely suggestion has been made that they accused Paul of taking the special offering for his own benefit. They certainly questioned the validity of his ministry as an apostle. Their insults caused Paul much pain (2:1-5).

Relevance for Today

Second Corinthians breathes with the inspiration of the Holy Spirit. It comes from the heart of a great church leader. It is addressed to specific situations in the life of a church. It is not surprising, then, that it speaks directly to some key issues in churches today.

Suffering.—Every person experiences pain and distress in life. Suffering is a major theme of 2 Corinthians. Paul's inspired understanding of suffering speaks to every Christian. The most important point is that God gives the comfort (1:3-6) and strength (12:7-10) necessary to turn misery into ministry. Ministry, if it is true to Christ, requires suffering. Suffering equips for ministry. It puts God's servant in touch with his own weakness, the strength of God, and the hurt of others.

Ministry.—What is the ministry of the church? of a church leader? of a church member? These questions are as pressing today as they were in first-century Corinth. Paul's answer is that the church is a ministry of reconciliation that invites persons to participate in the new creation in Christ. Such a ministry requires that the church (vocational ministers and lay ministers) model the Christ way of life. Ministry is not building up one's own power, authority, and profit (5:12; 12:14-18). It is giving self in suffering love for others (6:4-10; 11:23-29). It is emptying self to make life available as a vessel for God's power (4:7). It is carrying forward the ministry of Christ, and it must bear the marks of Christ. It is God, not our own ability that makes us competent to minister (3:4-6).

Leadership and authority.—What kind of leadership does a church need? How does a Christian lead other Christians? What authority guides a church? Pastors, staff, officers, and members struggle with these questions all the time. Traditional authorities in society have lost their grip. Confused people tend to follow strong authoritarian leaders. But should church members surrender their freedom and responsibility to super leaders or cult heroes (11:5) who promise visible proof of success? This was the danger at Corinth (11:19-21; 12:11).

Paul offered instead the pattern of Christlike leadership (12:12-19; 12:1-10). He aimed not to impress but to serve and build up. He preferred to lead gently, even at the risk of appearing weak; but he could give strong direction when that was needed. Christian leadership is flexible, but it is always centered around the example of Christ. The authority to lead comes only by sharing in the suffering of Christ.

The nature of the gospel.—Human nature resists the implications of the gospel. There is a strong tendency to substitute schemes of human effort (11:3-4). Men twist Christ and the cross to include their pet theories. The heart of Paul's message to Corinth is that God reconciles the world to himself in Christ, dealing with the problem of sin and accomplishing a new act of creation (4:3-6; 5:14-17). Those who are newly created in Christ have a new nature. The ways of the world and the idols of the world can no longer direct their lives (6:14 to 7:1).

Christian giving.—Like ancient Corinth, our culture is characterized by luxury, materialism, and inequality. Many in the world have too little. Some have more than enough. Paul put a strong emphasis on giving (chaps. 8—9). God calls his people to serve him by meeting the needs of others. Christian ministry is specific, and it costs money. The church need not hesitate to challenge Christians to give their money, but the key is to give our own selves first. Stewardship is based on the fact that God is a generous provider. Everything we have comes from him. He can continue to supply our needs as we give to others.

The Apostle Confident But Concerned
1:1 to 2:17

More Than Just a Greeting (1:1-2)

Ancient letters followed a standard form, just as letters do today. We put the signature at the end, but the writer of New Testament times started by identifying himself and then naming his readers. Next he expressed some prayer or wish for the recipients. With Paul this was more than a formality. He used every line to express a message of faith. His greeting tells us a lot about himself, his readers, and the good news he preached.

Paul usually identified himself as an apostle of Jesus Christ. "Apostle" is a key word because Paul was contending with false teachers in Corinth who claimed to be apostles and challenged Paul's qualifications. The word itself comes from a Greek word meaning "send for a particular purpose." Thus it means "one sent" or "one commissioned." The title was reserved for those who had experienced the risen Lord and who had been directly commissioned by him. Paul was one who was sent on special assignment by God. As we shall see later, it was especially important for him to stress this to the church at Corinth, where his authority had been questioned.

He also introduced the associate who was with him when he wrote. Timothy was not an apostle, but he was a fellow believer and therefore a brother. He had been Paul's messenger to Corinth earlier (1 Cor. 4:17).

The readers are introduced too. Not only the Corinthians, but all the Christians in Achaia, the Roman province south of Macedonia, are included. Paul reminded them that they were "saints," meaning holy people, people set apart as God's possession. The church is first of all God's church.

In all his letters, Paul replaced the usual Greek word for "greeting" with a similar word meaning "grace." It was a major theme for Paul and one of the great words of the New Testament. Referring to all that God does to save sinners, "grace" indicates unmerited favor.

In spite of man's sin, God gives his love. In spite of man's unrighteousness, God makes him righteous. God gives this undeserved gift because of his love and his sovereign power. Man cannot bring it about by his effort. He can only receive it by faith.

"Peace" was a common Jewish greeting. In the New Testament it has a deeper meaning. Originally it meant freedom from conflict both internal and external. In this sense it is the opposite of the feeling Paul expressed in 2 Corinthians 7:5: "Our bodies had no rest but we were afflicted at every turn—fighting without and fear within." In the fuller sense it describes all the blessings of salvation.

The Ministry of Suffering (1:3-11)

As Paul introduced his theme, the very first paragraph shows the rich meaning and intense feeling that characterizes 2 Corinthians. The passage is a doxology that describes both comfort and suffering.

The emphasis is on God. He is the "God . . . of our Lord Jesus Christ" (v. 3). He is like Jesus, but he is more than Jesus. He is his "Father." God is specifically known as "the Father of mercies," the Hebrew way of saying merciful Father, and as "the God of all comfort," the one whose comfort meets every need.

Paul, and those who join with him in Christian service, experience many difficulties. But God provides strength in each case. This strength becomes a rich resource for ministering to others. Paul viewed his suffering not as misery but ministry. He came to this conviction through his own experience of suffering (see 12:7-10).

Much of the comfort Paul received came from knowing that his suffering was related to "Christ's sufferings." The Jews expected the time of the Messiah to be preceded by the suffering of his people. Jesus, however, suffered for his people. Those whom he called to follow him also suffered in order to bless others. With this profound view of suffering Paul could encourage the Corinthians. He had great hope for them because he knew their sufferings would lead to their greater strength in the future.

Paul firmly believed that suffering is a part of ministry. This led him to point to his own suffering to provide an example for the Corinthians and to witness to God's deliverance. Something terrible had happened to him in Asia (the Roman province around Ephesus). No details are given, but the best theory is that Paul was referring to some serious physical threat. It may have been the attack on his ministry at Ephesus (Acts 19:21 to 20:1; 20:19; 1 Cor. 15:32) or some later crisis. Clearly his life was in danger.

Such a crisis had a purpose for one who lived by faith. It led him to trust God, not himself. A man has no power in the face of death, but God is the one "who raises the dead" (v. 9). He delivered Paul from death that time and would again. When Paul did come to die he would hope in God and in the resurrection, not in some possibility of escape.

Another purpose of suffering—and another reason for sharing it with his friends—was the opportunity for partnership in prayer. The Corinthians were not strong Christians, yet Paul confessed that he valued their help. By means of prayer, the weakest Christian can help the greatest Christian. The prayers of the Corinthians helped Paul, and his blessings yielded joy and gratitude in their lives. In this sense intercessory prayer is an investment that pays dividends for the pray-ers as well as the prayed-for. The more prayer is offered, the more thanksgiving there will be when the prayer is answered.

Something to Be Proud Of (1:12-14)

Verse 12 looks back to verse 11. Paul had a right to ask for the prayers of the Corinthians because his conscience was clear about his behavior toward them. He spoke of a "boast." This word and its related forms occur twenty-nine times in 2 Corinthians, more than in all the rest of the New Testament. It is a theme that runs throughout the book. Because others were boasting, Paul felt that he must engage in this foolish approach to set the record straight. He stressed the propriety of his conduct toward the Corinthians because it had been questioned by his critics. His enemies had been saying that Paul did not really mean the things he said, so he affirmed that his present writing was clear and understandable. The Corinthians already knew enough to know his sincerity. They had better opportunity than most to know his character. He had been with them many months. He expressed confidence that when they all stood before their Lord, they would be proud of each other.

Dependable Promises (1:15-22)

At the end of 1 Corinthians (16:5-7) Paul had announced a visit to Corinth after he passed through Macedonia. Later he changed his mind and planned two visits, one going to and one coming from

Macedonia. When he learned of their hostility toward him, he again changed his plans. A second visit would only bring added pain (2:1-11). The Corinthians thought, or were likely to think, that Paul was wishy-washy. If he were really inconsistent, then the flaw could extend to his preaching as well. Such an inference was unthinkable to Paul.

Not only was Paul's preaching consistent and positive; it was concerned with these very characteristics in Christ himself. God had promised salvation to his people, and Christ had fulfilled that promise. Paul might have been changeable about his travel plans, but his strategy was consistent with the gospel. It was always based on the question, "What is the most redemptive thing to do in this situation?" The appropriate action might change, but the principle did not. Paul always said yes to the redemptive purpose of God, just as Christ always says yes to the salvation of his people. It is this consistency at a deeper level to which Paul pointed. With his lips and his life he said "Amen" to the fact that God had kept his word through Christ.

Paul's faithfulness to the gospel was not a result of his own accomplishment. God had "commissioned" him (literally "anointed"). The presence of God's Spirit in his life witnessed to his inheritance in the kingdom of God and enabled him to serve God.

Determined to Do No Harm (1:23 to 2:4)

After his defense of his gospel, Paul returned to the immediate question about his change of plans. It was for the Corinthians' benefit. He felt it was so important to emphasize this that he was willing to call God as a witness against him if he were not telling the truth. But, since he had spoken so strongly, he did not want the Corinthians to think that he was claiming too much authority. He did not see himself as their lord. Rather, he was their fellow worker, and his aim was joy in their lives. Nor did he think they needed an authoritarian leader, for they were firm in their faith.

The decision not to make another visit, then, was to avoid causing pain to the church. The last visit had done this, and Paul saw no reason to do it again. For him to hurt the Corinthians would be to hurt himself. They were his source of joy. If he caused them sorrow, they could not make him glad.

Instead of making a second, painful visit, Paul had written a painful letter, perhaps the one included in 2 Corinthians 10—13. Even this had been difficult for him, and he wanted them to know that he did it out of love to restore the joy that should exist in their relationship.

How to Treat the Troublemaker (2:5-11)

Here Paul began to speak of the specific problem between him and the Corinthian church. He wrote with such tact and restraint that he did not give enough details to explain the problem to the modern reader. All we know for sure is that one man had done something that hurt the whole church as well as Paul himself. Paul mentioned the offense in 7:12. There he indicated that he did not want to focus on the wrongdoer or the one hurt. He wanted to influence the attitude of the whole church. The most likely explanation of all this is that it was Paul himself who was wronged by a member of the church who questioned his authority as an apostle, his integrity, and perhaps his motives regarding money (12:14-18).

The majority in the church had already punished the offender in some way. Paul felt this was enough. He should now be forgiven or else he might be overcome by his sorrow. Paul wanted them to know that he joined in forgiving this person. His purpose in writing the letter of rebuke had been accomplished. He had simply wanted to be sure that they were still obedient to Christ and that the integrity of his ministry was recognized. In forgiving the offender he was acknowledging that Christ was present in the situation, and he was seeking the welfare of the church. Not to forgive would be to let Satan win the war after they had already won the battle. The ancient preacher Chrysostom said, "Some Satan destroys through sin, others through the unmeasured sorrow following on repentance for it . . . conquering us with our own weapons!" [1]

Paul's Quest for Titus (2:12-13)

Paul's pattern in this letter was to state a fact about his personal history and then to launch a discussion of some larger idea. Here he was about to plunge into an extended discussion of his ministry as an apostle, but his starting point was once again a bit of personal experience. He had come to Troas to preach the gospel and had found the opportunity to be open. However, he was awaiting the return of Titus. When he did not find him, his anxiety about this moved him to go on to Macedonia to meet his associate. His concern as a pastor overcame his concern as an evangelist.

God's Victory March (2:14-17)

Instead of going on to describe their reunion, Paul broke into an exclamation of praise for the way God worked in their ministry. Not until 7:5 did he return to the subject of his trip to Macedonia. There he told how Titus met him in Macedonia with joyful news from Corinth. The thought of that joy seemed to be in Paul's mind as he began his discourse on ministry in verse 14.

The news that the Corinthians had repented of their hard feelings (7:9) and felt kindly toward him (7:7) moved Paul to rejoice at the way God worked in his ministry. He portrayed God as a Roman general returning in triumph with a parade of captives to prove his victory. Paul regarded himself as one taken captive by God, a trophy of his saving power. His missionary journeys were occasions when God led him from one place to another. And just as burning incense filled the air for the Roman victory parades, Paul's ministry was the aroma of Christ to the people he encountered.

Paul contrasted this profound view of ministry with the approach taken by some, perhaps those who criticized him at Corinth. They were peddlers of God's message. The word for peddler suggested a wine merchant who watered down his product and could be translated "huckster." They sought their own advantage, neglecting the people and altering the message to make their sales on any terms that would profit them. Paul, on the other hand, was a sincere representative of Christ accredited by God himself.

The Grandeur and Grief of Ministry
3:1 to 5:10

Living Letters (3:1-3)

Paul had just poured out his heart in praise for what God had done in his ministry. He had also contrasted his ministry with others who were not sincere. But he did not want anyone to think he was writing a letter of recommendation for himself. Letters of introduction were common in the early church as Christians traveled about. The trouble-

makers who had come to Corinth apparently had such letters, and
they may have objected that Paul did not have them. Paul, however,
had something better. His ministry to the people of Corinth had made
a direct impression on their lives. They of all people did not need
anyone to vouch for Paul. They were living proof for all to see that
Paul was a true minister.

Competent Ministry (3:4-6)

Paul was very confident, not of himself but of God. He did not
feel he could claim authority on his own. He had a sense of competence
that came from being a minister of the new covenant, the new relationship between God and man created by Christ. A minister who
offers such a covenant has a distinct advantage over those who presented the old covenant or those who preach any mechanical, legalistic
faith. Those all rest on words and rules with their deadening effect.
The new covenant is the work of the Spirit, and he provides the
life needed for a new creation.

The word "minister" was an important one for Paul. Either the
noun or the verb or the broader term "ministry" are found in all of
Paul's letters except those to the Thessalonians. The Greek word has
been carried over into English in our word "deacon." It means servant.
It is the same word Jesus used of himself as one who came to minister
(Mark 10:45). In various forms it occurs often in 2 Corinthians. In
5:18 it is the "ministry of reconciliation." It does not describe a special
office, either "minister" in the modern professional sense or "deacon"
in the sense of a lay officer of the church. Rather, it describes the
function of service and the role of a servant.

Paul introduced the contrast between the covenants here because
his critics at Corinth took pride in their Jewish background and because the contrast was a basic feature of his own experience. In Romans
7 and 8 he described how the law had only served to expose his
helplessness, while Christ had delivered him and given him new life.

The Fading Glory of the Law (3:7-11)

Paul continued to discuss the superior content of his ministry by
contrasting Moses and the law with Christ and the Spirit. Moses had
introduced a new relationship between God and man. The Revised
Standard Version calls it a "dispensation," but the word is literally
"ministry" or "service." Paul called it a ministry of death (v. 7) and

condemnation (v. 9). This does not mean that the law was evil. On
the contrary, God gave it and Paul had been devoted to it. But he
knew that it did not bring life. It was a temporary stage which had
to be replaced by something permanent. It was carved on stone (v.
7) and had only external authority. What was needed was a living,
spiritual covenant that had inner force in people's lives. The old covenant had a certain splendor and glory. Moses' face shone with the
radiance of his encounter with God, but the glow was only temporary.

The Life-changing Glory of Christ (3:12-18)

The minister of the new covenant is in a much better position
than Moses. Moses put a veil over his face because it shone (Ex. 34:33-
35). The Exodus account does not specify why he did this, but Paul
explained that he did not want them to see the fading away of the
glow. Paul went on to apply the idea of the veil to what happened
when the people of Israel read the law in his own day. The lack of
God's living presence in their hearts made them unable to see what
God wanted to reveal. This veil or obstacle is removed when people
turn to the Lord. "The Lord"—that is, Christ—"is the Spirit" (v. 17).
This does not mean there is no difference between Christ and the
Holy Spirit. It means the Lord acts through the Spirit. The Spirit
liberates persons so they can receive God's revelation. This is what
the law lacked. Moses had only the written law and a brief, fading
glimpse of glory. Christ has the life-changing Spirit and an ever-in-
creasing glory.

The Ministry of Light (4:1-6)

When Paul said "therefore," he was pointing back to all he had
just written about the glory of ministry in the new covenant. Because
he had such confidence in his gospel and in the mercy of God, Paul
could not be discouraged, even though he had many problems that
could have discouraged him.

Neither did Paul let difficulties pressure him into taking shortcuts
in the ministry. Other teachers at Corinth may have seemed to present
a more popular approach to the faith. Ministers, like other people,
are sometimes tempted to use questionable methods or to water down
their message to make it more acceptable. Paul was determined not
to do this. His Lord and his gospel demanded that he be open and
truthful. His appeal was to the conscience, not to lower instincts.

Paul recognized that not everyone will understand and accept the gospel. Some are perishing in unbelief and cannot see the light of Christ because they are spiritually blind. Satan is the god of this age, not a true god but one people have mistaken for their god. Satan is a deceiver, and he works to keep people from seeing the truth.

This is the only place in Scripture where Satan is called "the god of this [age]" (the word is literally "age," not "world"). In Ephesians 2:2 he is called "the [ruler] of the power of the air." In John 12:31 he is "the ruler of this world." God has not surrendered control of his world to Satan, but men have used their free will to give him a measure of power. This corrupt rule is limited to this age, while God will rule for all the ages to come. Paul refers to Satan as a god because he is so regarded by his subjects and because he wanted to contrast him with the true God.

While Satan is a false god, Jesus is the very likeness of God. It is Jesus Christ the Lord who was the subject of Paul's preaching, not Paul himself. All that Paul wanted to say about himself was that he was a servant of Christ, dedicated to the welfare of the Corinthians. In Christ, God, who created light in the beginning, has given his people a light in their hearts which comes from his self-revelation in Christ. Paul agreed with John that those who have encountered Christ have beheld the glory of God (John 1:14,18; 14:9).

Treasure in Earthen Vessels (4:7-12)

In spite of Paul's glorious gospel, some at Corinth thought he was unimpressive. His experience was very different from theirs. He had suffered intense persecution, including imprisonment and stoning. Recently he had been near death again. The Corinthians had not faced such opposition. There was neither strong Jewish resistance nor pressure to worship Caesar at Corinth. If anything, the church was on too-good terms with its environment. It had many internal difficulties, but it had not been attacked from without. It was easy for them to look down on the battered apostle.

At this point in his letter Paul dealt with this difference in their experience. First he pointed out that a messenger such as he was a vessel carrying precious contents. The treasure of the gospel does not receive its value from its container. It derives its power from God, not from the vessel which is common clay. The treasure is something "we have"—that is, not just Paul, but all Christians. In this context it consists of "the knowledge of the glory of God in the face of [Jesus] Christ" (4:6). This is nothing less than the sum total of revelation and redemption. What unbelievable grace that it should have been placed in "earthen vessels"—that is, in the lives of ordinary Christians!

In the ancient world almost everything was stored in clay jars, including treasure. But it is a striking turn of thought for Paul to carry this image over to describe the life of a Christian witness. The Old Testament often describes human life in terms of earthenware vessels (Isa. 29:16; 30:14; 45:9; 64:8; Jer. 18:6; Lam. 4:2; Job 10:9). In these passages the vessel stands for the whole person, not just the physical body. The truth Paul drew from this was that there is "transcendent power" in the Christian's life. It does not come from the person but from God.

To show how the power of God works in spite of human frailty, he mentioned five crisis situations in which the frail vessel would have failed or broken except for strength from beyond. The first four may be drawn from the combat games of the arena and are progressive in intensity. They were Paul's way of saying, "Down but not out."

The first crisis is external pressure, in Paul's case persecution, but including "all things." In such situations we are "not forsaken." We are never without "a way of escape" (1 Cor. 10:13).

The second type of difficulty is inner perplexity, but this perplexity can never get us down. There is a play on words in the Greek text, for the term for "driven to despair" is an intensified form of the first word, "perplexed."

The third describes interpersonal conflict, "persecuted, but not forsaken." The language literally means "pursued," as a retreating warrior might be pursued by his foes. But even in such a dire strait, God continues to give support.

The fourth crisis is acute danger, "struck down, but not destroyed." The warrior is actually wounded and down, but he is not finished. God is still at work even in defeat and mortal danger.

The fifth image is impending death. Here Paul left his images and described his experience directly. All of life was a confrontation with death, but this was not tragedy. It was an opportunity for triumph as the life of Christ exerted "transcendent power" in the frail vessel.

Paul's sufferings had not defeated him. On the contrary, they were signs that the work of Christ was being accomplished through him.

Doing Christ's work had resulted in suffering, and the life of Christ in him had brought about his victory.

Verse 12, "So death is at work in us, but life in you," seems to refer to the fact that Paul and the Corinthians had different callings. He had been called to face the danger of death. They had been allowed to live without such suffering.

The Spirit of Faith (4:13-15)

Paul quoted the Greek version of Psalm 116:10, "I kept faith, therefore I spoke up, but I was greatly humiliated."[2] Like the psalmist, he bore witness to a faith that endured suffering. He also had something in common with the Corinthians. He and they would experience resurrection with Christ into the presence of God. Paul's suffering was for their sake, and the grace that flowed through his ministry would bring glory to God. Thus the frail vessel of earth would prove to be a carrier of heavenly treasure.

Preparation for Glory (4:16-18)

Paul's hope in Christ kept him from being discouraged. His inner life was gaining new strength from God. His temporary troubles were simply getting him ready for "an eternal weight of glory beyond all comparison" (v. 17). What God had in store for him was so great that it could not be described. It was vast and never-ending. Paul had no visible proof of this. He based his hope on unseen reality. Visible evidence could only be temporary. The unseen work of God is eternal.

Earthly Tent and Heavenly Home (5:1-5)

As Paul compared his fragile hold on life with the coming glory of resurrection, he returned to a theme prominent in his first letter (1 Cor. 15), the change that will take place in the believer's body. Our present physical life will someday end. This body is like a tent that will be taken down so that we can go home to our permanent house. We do not fear dismantling the tent because we have another, more permanent home. This heavenly dwelling is made by God and can also be compared to a garment. By striking the body-tent, death threatens to leave us unprotected and vulnerable. But moving into the heavenly dwelling wraps us in a new covering of life. We naturally experience anxiety as we face death, but we find strength in the promise of new life. God prepares us by giving us the Holy Spirit as an advance assurance of heavenly life.

At Home or Away (5:6-10)

Because Paul's security was in God, he could be confident even in the face of death. Life in this present body is like a trip away from home. Death is like returning home. Paul realized that being at home with God would be best, but he could give himself to life in the present by exercising faith and by doing what pleased God. Either way he knew that he was responsible to God for what he did in this life. His mind shifted from the vision of death as homecoming to death as judgment. Paul saw that Christ will be the judge of all. Even the great apostle must stand before the judgment seat. Paul clearly taught that we are saved by grace, through faith, not by our own accomplishments (Eph. 2:8-9); but he also knew that we are saved in order to do God's work (Eph. 2:10). When we appear before our Lord, some of our works will be seen to be unworthy. Others will receive his approval. This did not shake Paul's confidence in his relationship with Christ, but it made him aware of the need to live responsibly.

The Ministry of Reconciliation
5:11 to 7:16

The Motive and the Message (5:11-15)

Paul may have been speaking of his evangelistic ministry when he said, "We persuade men"; but it was more likely that he meant his effort to persuade the Corinthians of his sincerity. He had been criticized as being insincere. In response to this he had just revealed his constant awareness of God's purpose and judgment. It was characteristic of Paul that he always thought of God as seeing and knowing his every act.

The "fear of the Lord" is a prominent theme in the Old Testament. In Proverbs 1:7 it is said to be "the beginning of knowledge." It is the basic attitude of awe and reverence that puts life in proper perspective. It is a kind of energy that purifies and empowers life. It was this fear or holy respect that Paul produced as exhibit A to prove his sincerity. His true character was known to God, and he felt that the Corinthians were spiritually sensitive enough to know it too.

In saying this, Paul did not mean to be bragging. Rather, he was trying to meet a need in the lives of his friends. The critics had raised questions in their minds. They put the emphasis on their outward standing in the church; Paul put it on inner standing in relation to God. The motive was what counted, and God knew Paul's motives. The Corinthians needed to be reassured themselves, and they needed to have ammunition to counter the critics. Any doubt at this point would injure the effectiveness of Paul's message. This he wanted to avoid at all costs. Chapters 10—12 provided extensive details about Paul's concern at this point.

There is some question about the interpretation of verse 13. Was Paul being accused of indulging in excessive ecstatic experience? Many take it that way. However, a closer study of the Corinthian situation makes it more likely that Paul had refrained from public displays of such experience (1 Cor. 14:19). His critics, on the other hand, had joined in this popular activity at Corinth and thought Paul unspiritual because of his restraint. He answered that he did know what it meant to be beside himself with ecstasy, but this was only between him and God. In his relation with the people of the church, he found it more helpful to be in his right mind. This twofold concern with the glory of God and the good of the people is a constant theme of his ministry.

Verses 14-21 constitute one of the most important statements of the message of the gospel in all the New Testament. The controlling factor of his ministry, Paul emphasized, was the love of Christ as seen in his death. This was where he learned such dedication. By "the love of Christ controls us" Paul did not have in mind the impulse that sent him on his mission, but the restraint that kept him from seeking his own advantage and held him to the cross. The word for "control" has the sense of pressure which confines and restricts. Such a total commitment to the good of others kept him from doing anything that would falsify the gospel or hinder Christian growth.

In verse 15 the *motive* of Paul's ministry and his *message* are seen to be the same, for both flow from the cross. The death of Christ was the most important fact in Paul's thinking. It affected all people by making possible the most radical change in their lives. Paul saw Christ as the second Adam (Rom. 5:14-17), God's new beginning in the creation of humanity. As such, he was the representative of the human race. What happened to him happens to all in some sense. Those who accept their unity with him by faith take part in the death he died for them.

Death to sin and resurrection to new life become the pattern of their lives. They no longer live to serve themselves. To live for self is sin. They live for Christ, and thus for others. This is more than mere acceptance of an idea. It is participation in a new reality. So Paul saw his task as notifying all persons of this new possibility and enlisting them to join in experiencing it. The word "all" is prominent in verses 14-15, and it indicates the breadth of Paul's missionary goal.

The New Has Come (5:16-21)

Paul's critics judged him—and themselves—"from a human point of view," literally "by what he is in the flesh." They valued persons on the basis of outward appearances and superficial signs. He now told the Corinthians that such evaluations were sub-Christian. The merely human point of view missed what God was doing. Since Paul's conversion he did not see or evaluate people merely in terms of their human characteristics. He was concerned with their hearts and the work of the Spirit in their lives. Before conversion he saw Christ as the world saw him, a troublesome teacher who died a shameful death. This passage does not really tell us whether Paul ever saw Jesus during his earthly life, but it does not seem likely or Paul would probably have indicated it specifically.

The emphasis was on the present. As a believer in Christ Paul now knew him as the loving Savior who brings grace by his death and life by his resurrection. This statement does not mean that Paul had no interest in the earthly life of Jesus, simply that he now saw it from a new point of view. As a new person he saw with new eyes. This led to his overwhelming concern for others.

Verse 17, with its great "therefore," points back to what Paul said about Christ's dying for all and all dying with him (vv. 14-15). When Christ rose from the dead, the human race made a new start. All who are united with him by faith are part of this new creation. They are "in Christ," a term Paul used constantly throughout his letters to describe his relationship with Christ. It implied that those who exercise faith in Christ enter into a real, personal union with him. Because they participate in his death to sin, the old things have passed away. This is true even though the old order hangs on for a while. The new creation will not be fully revealed until the new heaven and the new earth appear; but for those who are in Christ, the new order has already begun.

The new creation is God's doing. Only the Creator of all things could bring about such a gracious change. He has accomplished the transformation through Christ, in whom Creator and humanity come together as one. Such a new creation, based as it is on union with Christ, requires that the hostility and separation between man and God be ended. This is the meaning of the word "reconciling." Verses 14-15 indicate that Christ's death and resurrection are the means of redemption. Verse 21 states that his atonement for sin is the basis of reconciliation. The phrase "God was in Christ reconciling" (v. 19) points to his incarnation and his divine-human nature as the channel of reconciliation.

The word "reconcile" occurs three times in various forms in verses 18-19. It is also found in Romans 5:10-11. A similar word, also translated "reconcile," is used in Ephesians 2:16 and Colossians 1:20. In all these cases the reference is to persons being reconciled to God. The emphasis is on something God does for humanity to overcome their hostility toward him.

Verse 19 restates the truth of verse 18 and adds the explanation, "not counting their trespasses against them." Reconciliation implies that a state of enmity had existed due to sin. "Trespasses" means violations of God's law or failures to do what is right. Such offenses God could have counted against mankind. Rather than do this, he overcame the enmity. Reconciliation requires effective treatment of the root cause of the hostility. This means that it is more than something that changes people's attitudes. It is something that God accomplishes that draws God to man and man to God. Certainly God loved us even before Christ died for us. He did not have to have his mind changed in order to become our friend. But God demanded holiness of us and rejected our sin. Something had to be done to remove that sin so that God could receive us and we could receive the love God has for us. To accomplish this, Christ took upon himself the judgment for our sin.

As a preacher and evangelist, Paul was not content to spell out a doctrine of reconciliation. He went on to make a forceful appeal. The reconciliation of man to God has been accomplished in Christ, but it must be known and accepted by man to become effective. Because of this, the work of God in reconciliation flowed into the ministry of Paul. His discussion of the doctrine of reconciliation was against the background of his discussion of his ministry. He was explaining what he was doing by explaining what God was doing.

God's appeal comes to persons through messengers like Paul, who are here called "ambassadors." This is a very meaningful word because the Greeks used it to describe an important official in the Roman Empire. Roman provinces that were peaceful were under the direct control of the emperor and his representative on the scene, called a legate or ambassador. He was the direct, personal representative of the emperor. When a country was in process of becoming a Roman province, the senate would send ten ambassadors to arrange the terms of peace. Thus an ambassador was one who brought former enemies into the family of Rome. Paul saw himself as the direct representative of God in foreign, hostile territory, inviting former enemies to come into God's family. It was up to him to represent his master in every way. The reputation of Christ and the church was in his hands. It was a great responsibility and a great privilege.

To reinforce his appeal, Paul restated the means and results of reconciliation in verse 21. It is made possible by Christ's remedy for sin. "Made him to be sin" means at least that God made Christ to bear the consequences of sin. But it is a daring phrase that may mean much more. In some mysterious sense the sinless Christ became identified with our sin so that we could become identified with his righteousness. As a result of this, those who are in Christ by faith "become the righteousness of God"—that is, they receive the benefits of God's righteousness. They take on the characteristics of Christ as he takes on their former characteristics as sinners. This is not just a label of righteousness. They become righteous as they are transformed into the image of Christ.

Servants of God in Every Way (6:1-10)

Chapter 6 continues the thought of 5:20. Paul was cooperating with God in a partnership of preaching. Both divine action and human witness are required to bring about reconciliation. The plea to the

Corinthians was that they not receive the grace of God in vain. Some of them might not have responded in faith to the message. But, more likely, Paul felt they were in danger of embracing a lesser substitute for the gospel of the cross.

Instead of this, he reminded them of the promise in Isaiah 49:8. The day of salvation had already come. The blessings of the kingdom were theirs. The present moment was the time to trust fully in God's redemption.

Paul again stressed the positive nature of his ministry. He was aware that some found fault with his work, but he did not give in to their criticism. He was confident that he had done nothing to hinder their faith. On the contrary, he had done everything as a servant of God; so all his experiences had worked to commend the gospel.

At this point Paul listed his sufferings, just as he did in 4:8-9. The very things that made him unimpressive to his critics were cited by him as ways of commending the gospel. His endurance bore witness to the patient suffering of Christ. "Endurance" is one of the key words of the New Testament. Paul had already used the verb form in 1:6 as he described the endurance of suffering which he and the Corinthians had in common. It occurs throughout Paul's writings, especially Romans and 2 Corinthians. It means constant strength under difficulty. Jesus gave it great emphasis (Luke 21:19; Mark 13:13; Matt. 10:22; 24:13). Early Christian writers often described it as the chief Christian virtue. It does not mean passive acceptance of difficulty but the transformation of trouble into victory. In modern terms it could be described as coping successfully with life.

Verses 4-5 set forth nine kinds of suffering in three groups of three each. The first set of difficulties are the conditions under which Paul worked. They described increasing degrees of difficulty. "Afflictions" was a word much used in the New Testament to describe the pressures or crushing burdens of life. "Burdens" literally meant necessities or things that cannot be avoided. "Calamities" literally meant a place that is too narrow. It describes those situations in life when there seems to be no way out.

The second triplet of troubles described the attacks Paul suffered from his opponents. "Beatings" were literally stripes from whips and rods with which Paul was beaten by his persecutors. "Imprisonments" referred to the times when Paul was actually put in jail. He knew the inside of prisons in Philippi, Jerusalem, Caesarea, Rome, and prob-

ably many other places before his life was over. "Tumults" meant
disorders and probably referred to the mob violence which Paul often
encountered.

The third set includes the hardships Paul accepted in doing the
work of a missionary. "Labors" described work to the point of exhaus-
tion. It was a term Paul often used to describe his work, and it is
almost synonymous with the Christian life in the New Testament.
"Watching" meant sleeplessness. Because of duty, discomfort, or danger, Paul spent some sleepless nights. These were times of prayer,
witness, and even singing (Acts 16:25, and the entire chapter, where
Paul's experience in prison at Philippi illustrated this whole list of
difficulties). "Hunger" described going without food because either
time or money was lacking. It probably did not mean fasting for religious purposes. Like Jesus and his disciples, Paul sometimes "had no
leisure even to eat" (Mark 6:31). Paul's response to these sufferings
turned defeat into triumph.

In verses 6-7 Paul listed some features of his ministry by which
he commended himself as a minister of the gospel. "Purity" described
the clean heart and clean hands necessary to carry the message of
the gospel. It described moral purity and integrity. "Knowledge" included not only understanding of the faith but also insight into people
and common sense about what to do. "Forbearance" referred to patience with people and control of one's temper. "Kindness" referred
to a sweet and gracious spirit which avoided harming others.

"The Holy Spirit," of course, is not a quality but the source of all
these qualities and the one who gives the needed wisdom and skill
for ministry. The phrase here might better be translated "a spirit
that is holy" or "holiness of spirit." "Genuine love" was love without
any pretense, the kind of love God showed. "Truthful speech," literally
"by the word of truth" or "the declaration of the truth" may refer
to the preaching of the gospel or to truthfulness in general.

"The power of God" was the ability and authority of the one who
sent him to do his work. This was a basic theme of the entire letter
as Paul contrasted God's strength with his own weakness. To conclude
his list, Paul testified that his equipment for ministry was complete.
He had "weapons of righteousness" which were both offensive (the
sword was held in the right hand) and defensive (the left hand held
the shield).

Verses 8-10 gave nine contrasting pairs of characteristics that described the two-sided nature of the ministry. There are many negative factors, but each was outweighed by the positive. Just as the experience of Christ included both cross and resurrection, the Christian life is full of shadows which witness to the light all around. "Dishonor" was the term used to describe loss of rights as a citizen. But as a citizen of the kingdom Paul had a higher honor than this world bestows.

"Ill repute" was the way many thought of Paul, but with God and God's people his reputation was entirely different. He and his fellow missionaries were looked upon as "imposters," a word meaning a wandering deceiver or seducer. To those who could recognize it, though, their message was truth itself. His enemies considered him an "unknown," but he was "well known" by those who received the gospel from him. He was constantly in danger of "dying," but he was more fully alive than most. He was "punished" or disciplined, yet it was never such as to bring his life to an end. He had ample reason to be "sorrowful," but nothing could take away his joy. He was "poor" in terms of earthly wealth, but he could share the true wealth of the Spirit with all who would receive it. He committed himself to a life of "having nothing," but in Christ everything belonged to him.

An Appeal to the Heart (6:11-13)

Now that he had spoken to his friends in such bold terms, he paused to ask for their response. He had been completely open with them. His open mouth had poured out the truth. His open heart had offered love to all who would respond. They, however, had not been so open. The problem had been their attitude, not any unwillingness on his part. Now he asked them as he would have asked his own children, "Widen your hearts also."

Caution Against Compromise (6:14 to 7:1)

In the middle of his appeal for open hearts, Paul turned aside to discuss the dangers of Christians getting too involved with pagan idol worshipers. Some think this passage was originally part of another letter to Corinth, perhaps the one mentioned in 1 Corinthians 5:9-13. But that letter clearly dealt with immoral Christians. This passage obviously refers to unbelievers. The basic idea is clear: There can be no partnership between those who follow Christ and those who are committed to false gods. The difference between Christianity and all other loyalties was as great as the difference between light and darkness. Christians cannot blend in with the patterns of the world because the world has different aims and different loyalties. Christians are different because of their relationship with God. The holy one is their Father, and he lives in them. Individually and as a church they are his temple.

Paul turned to the Old Testament to make his point. He cited Isaiah 52:11, where the prophet called the Israelites to leave Babylon with its spiritual uncleanness and return to the land of divine promise. He also pointed to other passages (2 Sam. 7:8,14; Isa. 43:6; Jer. 31:9) which showed that God's people are in a special relationship with God and can have no such relationship with the evil forces in the world. Christians in today's society, no less than in pagan Corinth, need this reminder to keep their lives clean and to live in dedication to God.

The Appeal Continued (7:2-4)

In chapter 7 Paul brought his conversation with the Corinthians to a climax. The mood was one of affirmation and joy. Like an evangelist pressing his invitation he said, "Open your hearts to us." The issues have been dealt with. There is no more reason for hard feelings. But Paul knew that broken relationships have to be mended slowly with love, so he spoke very tenderly to his flock. Reminding them that he had not done anything to hurt them, he also let them know that he was not criticizing them for the strain in their relationship.

The important point is in verse 3: He wanted to be in their hearts because they were in his heart. He was willing to die for them and he did not want to live without them. In verse 4 Paul affirmed his friends by stating his great confidence and pride in them. In spite of the suffering he had experienced for them, he felt only joy and comfort now.

Comforting News from Corinth (7:5-16)

At the height of his expression of joy Paul turned to explain how the change came about. He had already mentioned his anxious waiting for Titus to return from Corinth (2:12-13). Now he finished the story. He had suffered acute distress. On the outside opponents of the gospel resisted him. On the inside he was concerned about the problems

at Corinth. What saved him from this crisis was comfort given by
God (see 1:3-4). It had come, as spiritual help so often does, through
human means. Titus returned at last, and he brought good news.
The Corinthians wanted to be reconciled with Paul. They were sorry
about the problems that had occurred. They were enthusiastic about
setting things right. Paul's worry turned to rejoicing.

One of his concerns had been the harsh letter he had sent them.
Was it too strong? Would they be crushed? For a while he was sorry
he had written it, but no more. Now he knew it had provoked only
a temporary grief, a grief that had led them to repent. Because this
godly grief had led to a change for the better, neither he nor they
had any cause to regret it. This process was the opposite of the world's
grief over evil, which was despair with no hope of change. Because
of their strong desire for change, the Corinthians had proved that
things were right again. His letter and its results had helped the Corinthians to realize how much Paul meant to them.

Titus, as well as Paul, was relieved at the way things had turned
out. He had heard from Paul that the Corinthians were really all
right, but he was gratified to find that they lived up to Paul's high
estimation of them. Paul was glad they had justified his optimism.
Titus now shared Paul's love for them, and Paul was all joy and confidence.

Committed Resources

8:1 to 9:15

A Gracious Work (8:1-7)

Chapters 8 and 9 provide the most extensive teaching on stewardship to be found in the New Testament. They also show the brilliant
leadership of a great missionary statesman. According to Acts and
Galatians, Paul was called to be the apostle to the Gentiles. The Jewish
Christians, led by James, Peter, and John, recognized Paul's mission;
but they found it difficult to relate to Gentile Christians who did

not keep the law. When they conferred with Paul about his ministry, they requested one thing which would help to build a bridge between Jewish and Gentile Christians. They asked him to "remember the poor," and Paul was "eager to do" this (Gal. 2:6-10).

Because Jerusalem was a major city and a religious center, it attracted many poor people. A number of these had become Christians. Jewish persecution had increased the poverty of the churches in Palestine. Famine had struck the region (Acts 11:28). Paul led his Gentile mission churches to give offerings to be sent to their Jewish brothers. This told the Jews of the depth of Christianity among the Gentiles. It also reminded the Gentiles of their spiritual debt to the Jews who shared God's revelation with them.

Paul began his appeal by pointing to the example set by the churches of Macedonia (Philippi, Thessalonica, and Berea). Believers in that region had suffered intense persecution (Acts 16—17; Phil. 1:29; 1 Thess. 2:14). This would have affected them economically. The fact that they nevertheless contributed to the offering for Christians in Palestine Paul described as "the grace of God." (See also vv. 6-7.) This term was significant. Paul saw stewardship as one way the Christian expressed the grace of God. There was much more involved than just money. In fact, Paul never even used the term "money" in his entire discussion of the gift.

The Macedonian Christians did not have much money, but they had a lot of joy. This made them want to share. They volunteered to have a part in the offering and asked Paul for the privilege of giving. They gave out of proportion to the limited means they possessed. The key to their generosity was the fact that they had already given themselves to God and to Paul. When God already has a person's very self, giving is simply a decision about where to allocate what already belongs to God.

In the light of this moving example, Paul now urged the Corinthians to respond. Titus had already begun the offering at Corinth. The unhappiness in the church had delayed its completion. Paul reminded the Corinthians that they had excelled in other areas. Corinth was a prosperous city, and the Corinthians had not suffered persecution like the Macedonians. They should be able to do even more. They rejoiced in their knowledge and spiritual gifts, and Paul agreed that these were genuine. Now he asked them to excel in doing something for someone else.

The Why and How of Giving (8:8-24)

Paul did not want the Corinthians to think he was ordering them to give. Rather, he expected them to be motivated by the example of others because they already had a genuine Christian love. This led him to the very heart of the stewardship motive, the gift of God in Christ. The "gracious work" he was urging them to do was an expression of "the grace of our Lord Jesus Christ." Christ willingly gave himself, emptying himself of his divine wealth (Phil. 2:5-8) so his people could receive the riches of eternal life. Giving is not just one part of Christianity. It belongs to the very nature of the gospel itself. When anyone realizes what Christ did for his sake, his life will begin to flow in the direction of others.

Though he did not order them, Paul did not hesitate to give his friends advice about practical procedures in giving. He reminded them that they needed to finish what was begun a year before. It was not enough to have good intentions about giving. The attitude must become an act.

The guideline for giving was "according to what a man has." He who has much should give much. He who has only a little should give out of what he has. His little, like the widow's mite (Luke 21:1-4), becomes much in the sight of God. Paul was not asking them to reduce themselves to want. The goal was equality. Verse 15 quotes Exodus 16:18. The Israelites were not permitted to hoard excess manna, but no one was left with too little, either.

Helpers in Giving (8:16-24)

Paul also let the Corinthians know that Titus shared his pastoral concern for them. He was not just carrying out Paul's instructions; he was leading them in the fund-raising effort because he wanted to do it. This was not only to help the Jewish Christians. Paul and Titus were doing it out of concern for the Corinthians.

Paul also mentioned two others who were coming to Corinth with Titus. There were several reasons for this. One was social. Christ's ministers enjoy companionship in service, and the Corinthians would enjoy fellowship with these men. Another was strategic. These men were designated by the churches to share in the work of fund raising. "Messengers of the churches" (v. 23) is literally "apostles" or "sent ones" of the churches. They would inspire those who gave, and they would represent the Gentile churches when the gift was delivered to Jerusalem. A third reason was precautionary. Paul did not want anyone to suspect him or Titus of wrongdoing in handling money.

The two helpers were not named. It may be that they were not yet known at Corinth; therefore, their names would not have been important in the letter. It was specified that both were Christians of some reputation. One was known for his preaching (v. 18). Many commentators suggest that this was Luke. The other was recognized for his proven earnestness (v. 22). Together with Titus they were not only messengers of the churches, they were the glory of Christ—that is, they were involved in an enterprise that would manifest the glory of Christ. Paul challenged the Corinthians to prove their love, not just to him but to these trusted representatives and to their sister churches.

Planning for a Willing Gift (9:1-5)

Paul knew that the Corinthians were willing and ready to give an offering. He did not need to inform them or persuade them. But he did see the need to encourage them. Most Christians need all the help they can get to move from good intentions to action. The recent problems at Corinth had slowed the offering to a standstill, and Paul knew that a new start must be made if the task were to be accomplished. Some of this urgency was dictated by the time schedule and the need to coordinate with other churches and with Paul's travel plans.

The apostle had used the example of the Corinthians to inspire the Macedonians, just as he used the Macedonians' generosity to inspire the Corinthians. He stated this to remind them that they had a responsibility to live up to. He also wanted to give them enough time to act freely and avoid the pressure of a last-minute drive.

The Theology of Giving (9:6-15)

Paul also gave a challenge about the spirit in which the gift is to be made. It should be given bountifully. The principle of planting and harvest applies to the whole Christian faith. Generous giving yields generous results. It should be given cheerfully. The inner attitude is as important to God as the outward gift. The Greek version of Proverbs 22:9 says that "God loves a cheerful giver."

Christian giving is based on the biblical understanding of God. If

God is a miser, then people need to hang on to what they have. But the fact is that God is a generous provider. Everything anybody has comes from him, and he will continue to supply their needs. Verse 9 quotes Psalm 112:9. Since God "scatters abroad" and "gives to the poor," his people can both trust him and follow his example.

Paul described a balance of grace somewhat like the balance of nature. As long as each member of the system is functioning properly, the needs of all are met. God supplies the needs of all people. People give to God by giving to one another. The giver is strengthened, the recipient is helped, and God is glorified. Gratitude flows to both God and man. When Paul thought of this marvelous economy of grace, he shouted, "Thanks be to God for his inexpressible gift!"

Confrontation with the Critics

10:1 to 13:14

The Potential for Boldness (10:1-6)

Paul's statement here implied that he was being criticized as a coward. His critics said that he was bold when he wrote from afar but humble when present in person. Paul's response was to appeal to the meekness and gentleness of Christ. That was the way he wanted to deal with people. So he pled with the Corinthians not to force him to use strong tactics when he came, but he let them know that he was fully prepared to use his strength if necessary.

He went on to show the difference between his kind of strength and that of his critics. They accused Paul of being "worldly" (literally "fleshly"). Like the gnostic heretics who came later, they prided themselves on being spiritual. Paul acknowledged that all of us live in the flesh, the realm of human weakness; but he insisted that his ministry was carried out on spiritual lines. It was a spiritual warfare, and Paul had the necessary weapons to win. He could deal with the arguments, pride, and rebellious thoughts of the enemy. He wanted everyone to understand that he would discipline those who had not been obedient to Christ.

Asserting Authority (10:7-11)

Paul challenged them to look at the facts as they knew them, not at what others said. The false teachers claimed to belong to Christ in a unique way. There was even a "Christ party" in Corinth (1 Cor. 1:12). But if they would only think back to their experience with Paul, they would know that Paul belonged to Christ if anyone did. He had no fear that he would claim too much in his letters and then not be able to live up to it in person. His letters might seem strong at times, but they were not just an empty show of force. The false apostles were saying, "Oh, his letters are fierce, but when you hear him in person he is unimpressive." Such accusations did not intimidate Paul. He knew that his conduct in person would match his words, and the Corinthians needed to remember that this was the case.

The Measure of a Man (10:12-18)

Paul did not intend to get into a contest of comparing himself with the false apostles. They compared themselves with each other and their own standards. Paul knew that this was an unwise course for a servant of Christ. Taking his cue from the word "measure" in verse 12, Paul went on to speak of "limits" (literally "measures") in verses 13 and 15. The critics questioned Paul's right to minister in Corinth. They wanted to declare the area "off limits" to him. Paul recognized that God had set some limits to his ministry. He was to go to the Gentiles and to preach in new mission fields. Corinth came well within those guidelines. He had been the first to open the work there. He was not overreaching himself to go to Corinth. He wanted to enlarge the work there and go on to other new fields. He would not, like the false apostles, be working in someone else's field. And, lest he seem to be in a contest of self-glorification with the critics, he reminded them all that the only proper glorying was in the Lord. It was God's commendation, not his own or any other person's, that mattered.

The Threat of the Super Apostles (11:1-6)

Paul now asked his readers to indulge him in some momentary foolishness for the sake of argument. In effect he was saying, "I'll play their little game." He did not want to boast or compare, but if that was what they wanted, he would show them he could do it better than they.

Although he feigned foolishness, Paul was really very serious. With deep feeling he told them that their relationship to Christ was a sacred marriage. This relationship had been threatened by the false teachers who had undermined their devotion to Christ just as the serpent seduced Eve. Such teachers talked about Christ, but their presentation of him was as though they were talking about a different Jesus. Their spirit and their gospel were different from Paul's, and he was disappointed that they were so easily misled.

Paul boldly rejected the idea that he was inferior to the false teachers. He called them—and perhaps they called themselves—"superlative apostles." They accused him of being unskilled, or a layman in speaking. The Greeks valued gifts of speech, and these teachers may have been trained in oratory. But Paul knew, and the Corinthians had reason to know, that he was highly skilled in knowledge. Even if he was a poor speaker by their standards, he knew what he was talking about.

Paul's Refusal of Money (11:7-11)

When Paul came to Corinth he worked as a tentmaker with Aquila and Priscilla (Acts 18:1-3). It was customary for Jewish teachers to support themselves by a trade, but the Greeks considered manual labor beneath the dignity of a teacher. The right of missionaries to be supported by the churches was clear to Paul, but he took special care at Corinth not to depend on the church financially (1 Cor. 9:6-15). He also accepted support from the churches of Macedonia rather than burden the Corinthians. His critics seem to have contended that these practices were not dignified enough for a true apostle and perhaps that they were a disgrace to the church. It was not from lack of love for the Corinthians that Paul refused their money. The very opposite was true.

Apostles in Disguise (11:12-15)

Paul's reason for consistently refusing financial support from the Corinthians was to show the contrast between himself and the false teachers. They claimed to be equal to Paul or superior, yet they encouraged the Corinthians to support them financially. Paul knew that this put them at a disadvantage. His strongest attack on them came in verse 13. They were "false prophets, deceitful workmen, disguising themselves as apostles of Christ." Worse still, this behavior proved that they were servants of Satan, not apostles of Christ. Like Satan, they disguised themselves with the appearance of righteousness. Their future fate, Paul warned, would be what was appropriate for such deeds.

Paul's Tactics and Theirs (11:16-21*a*)

Paul did not want to be considered foolish; but since he was so accused, he intended to act the part to make his point. He said in effect, "This will sound foolish, but it has a good purpose; so listen to me." This boastful role had no divine authority in Paul's view. But as long as that was the game his opponents were playing, he would show that he could beat them by their own rules. There was one important difference. They boasted of worldly things. Paul boasted of his sufferings.

The Corinthians, Paul noted, had shown a willingness to be led by such aggressive, authoritarian tactics. He sarcastically called them wise because his approach had been termed foolish. The false teachers had made slaves of them, had taken their money, and had humiliated them (the meaning of the reference to a slap in the face). If refusing to use such high-handed leadership was weakness, then Paul pled guilty to weakness.

The Credentials of Christ's Servant (11:21*b*-29)

Paul now showed that he could match the "superlative apostles" in a bragging match. In the words of a popular song, "Anything you can do, I can do better." They boasted of being Hebrews, those who spoke the language of their ancestors and read the sacred writings. They were Israelites, members of the chosen nation. They were heirs of Abraham and therefore to the promises made to him. But Paul was all of these, too.

They called themselves servants of Christ. Here Paul not only matched them; he went far beyond them. The evidence he listed was not a string of victories; it was a list of hardships suffered. He, and not they, showed the true marks of a servant of Christ, his sufferings. Most of the occasions listed do not appear in the book of Acts, which gives only a partial history of Paul's career. Verses 23-27 list the many forms of persecution he suffered, most of which came from his own people, the Jewish religious leaders. Verses 28-29 tell of another kind of suffering, the pressures of a pastor-evangelist as he cared for his churches. Paul agonized daily with his converts as they encountered difficulties.

This, Paul said, was the kind of boasting an apostle should do. He must tell of his weakness because that was where the strength of God touched the needs of people. Paul gave one more example, one which must have been well known to his friends (see Acts 9:19-24). The picture of Paul being hidden in a basket and smuggled out of Damascus was not heroic. It was actually humorous. But it indicated the courage and humility of the great apostle and the providence of God in his life.

Made Perfect in Weakness (12:1-10)

Paul's boasting now extended to spiritual experience. The Corinthians may have felt that a spiritual leader should be able to point to unusual visions and mystical experiences as qualifications. The false apostles may have claimed such experiences themselves. In any case, Paul let them know that he had experienced such a vision; but he made it clear that this was not the key to his effectiveness as a minister.

He referred to himself simply as "a man in Christ" to soften the element of boasting and to show how different that experience was from his usual experience. The incident had occurred fourteen years before, around A.D. 41. Paul had probably been a Christian for about seven years at the time. It must have been a crucial point in his life.

He was caught up to "the third heaven." Jewish thought speculated that there were levels of heaven, sometimes as many as seven. Third heaven here probably refers to the highest level. So strange was the experience that Paul did not know whether he went there physically or whether he was somehow separated from his body. The realm to which he went is also called "Paradise," a term borrowed from the Persians which means a park or a garden.

Paul was very reserved about the details of his experience. This was in line with the whole emphasis of the Bible, which avoids giving details about heaven and the spiritual order. He continued to speak of his experience as though it had happened to someone else. Concerning himself, he would only speak of his weaknesses, for it was there that he felt the real point of his ministry was to be found. He would not carry his boasting game to the point of boasting about his private spiritual experience. He wished to be evaluated on the basis of what others experienced in his life. He also knew that he was called to preach Christ and not visions.

There was a danger that such sublime spiritual experience would go to Paul's head. But God was at work in Paul's life to prevent that. He was given a "thorn in the flesh" which served as "a messenger of Satan" to prevent any unreal spiritual elation. We do not know the exact nature of this thorn. Some speculate that it may have been mental and spiritual anguish arising from his hardships or his grief over having persecuted the church. They point to the fact that the words could be translated "for the flesh," and Paul uses flesh for human nature in general. But most interpreters take the phrase more naturally and literally and conclude that Paul meant a physical ailment. Their guesses include epilepsy (because of his visions), malaria (because it was common in the regions where he traveled), and eye trouble (because Paul wrote with large letters in Galatians 6:11). Whatever the thorn was, the lesson Paul learned is clear. He asked God to remove it, but God did not. He wanted Paul to depend on his grace, not on Paul's own strength. He could affirm his disabilities because they were channels of God's power.

Enough of Such Talk (12:11-13)

Having spoken so much of himself, Paul cried out, "This is foolish!" He only resorted to this approach because the Corinthians required it to be able to get Paul's point. This grieved him because the Corinthians should have recognized what Paul had done for them. Even if he were nothing, he had ministered to them in ways the false apostles had not. The sacrifices he made and the changes in their lives were "the signs of a true apostle." In addition, there had been miracles or mighty works. Paul had done everything for them except take their money.

I Will Not Be a Burden (12:14-18)

Even though he had been criticized for not accepting support at Corinth, Paul did not intend to change his stand even when he made his next visit. The motivation of his ministry was not gain but grace. He wanted to give to them without thought of receiving. He found it ironic that this was interpreted as lack of love and even trickery. He questioned them closely to make them see that there was no evidence for the charge. Even the helpers he sent to Corinth did not take advantage of the people. Paul had been consistent in his policy.

A Pastor's Concern (12:19-21)

At this point Paul spoke of his motives for this discussion. He was not trying to defend himself to the people. He was declaring himself before God, counting on his testimony to strengthen the Corinthians. Underlying his effort was a deep fear that he would get to Corinth and find them in the grip of negative attitudes and actions. This list of evils will sound very familiar to anyone who has ever been in an angry, divided church.

Paul listed eight kinds of sin which he feared might exist at Corinth. The list was similar to other descriptions in Paul's letters, especially Galatians 5:19-21, where the same words for quarreling, jealousy, anger, and selfishness are found among the works of the flesh. The eight here seem to be grouped in four pairs. "Quarreling" is strife or rivalry. "Jealousy" is a mean spirit that begrudges the good of others. "Anger" is a word that describes outbursts of temper. "Selfishness" is the spirit that seeks one's own gain without thought of service to others. "Slander" refers to open verbal attacks. "Gossip" means whispering or talking about someone behind his back. "Conceit" is building up an inflated opinion about oneself. "Disorder" is a situation which has gotten out of hand because people act without thought of the common good. It has the idea of tumult or anarchy.

Paul could see himself grief-stricken as he met friends who had not repented of their sins. This would mean that they were once again living the old, pagan way of life. "Impurity" refers to uncleanness of any kind. "Immorality" is literally fornication or improper sexual relations. This was a persistent evil in such a pagan city as Corinth. "Licentiousness" means deliberate defiance of public decency. These are also works of the flesh which Paul named in Galatians 5:19. Hopefully, this vivid picture of what could happen would surely help it not to happen.

Words of Warning (13:1-4)

Now that Paul was about to visit for the third time, he issued a stern warning. He cited Old Testament law to show that two or three witnesses served to establish charges. This seemed to mean that he intended to conduct a thorough investigation and discipline wrongdoers in the church. If anyone doubted whether Paul spoke with authority, he now intended to show such authority. He had been

weak as Christ was weak on the cross. But he could also show the
strength of him who lives by the power of God.

Meeting the Test (13:5-10)

To those who had been judging him, Paul said, "Examine yourselves" and "Test yourselves." The real question for them was not
Paul's validity as an apostle but their own relationship with Christ.
If Christ was not in them, then they had failed the only test that
mattered. Paul wanted to be proved right himself, but he was more
concerned that they pass, even if he seemed to fail. If they heeded
his warning and corrected their ways, he would not have a chance
to come and prove his strength by disciplining them. But he would
be glad if that happened. The noun "improvement" in verse 9 is
the same word used as a verb in verse 11, "Mend your ways." He
had been accused of writing strong words and being weak in person.
Still he wrote this warning so he would not have to be severe in
using his authority. After all, the point of that authority was to build
up, not to tear down.

A Parting Plea (13:11-13)

The word for "mend" used in verse 11 (also in verse 9) is the same
word used in Mark 1:19 of James and John mending nets. When the
Corinthians had made things right on the human level, they would
enjoy fellowship with "the God of love and peace" on the divine
level. One sign of such love and peace was the custom of giving a
kiss in greeting, a practice the Christians took from the Jews. In the
worship of the synagogues and churches, men exchanged the greeting
kiss with men and women with women. It was a sign of putting away
wrongdoing and being reconciled with each other. It was most often
done in connection with the Lord's Supper. Paul closed by sending
greetings from "All the saints"—that is, all the believers with whom
he was in contact.

A Threefold Blessing (13:14)

The last sentence of the letter is a beautiful prayer which has become a familiar benediction in public worship. Paul's usual benediction is shorter: "The grace of our Lord Jesus Christ be with you"
(1 Thess. 5:28). Here, however, he added a blessing from God the
Father and the Holy Spirit, making this a clear reference to the three

persons of the Trinity. This longer blessing was appropriate for a
church that desperately needed more of God's love and more of the
fellowship of the Holy Spirit.

Notes

1. Quoted in R. V. G. Tasker, *The Second Epistle of Paul to the Corinthians,*
"Tyndale New Testament Commentaries," vol. 8 (Grand Rapids: William B.
Eerdmans Publishing Company, 1958), p. 55.

2. Translation of George Beasley-Murray, *Broadman Bible Commentary,*
vol. 11 (Nashville: Broadman Press, 1971), p. 31.

GALATIANS

Introduction

Galatians surely ranks as one of the most important books of the New Testament. It is crucial for understanding Paul. Written in the heat of one of his most important battles, it gives us vital insights into the mind and heart of the apostle. It is basic for understanding Christian faith, for it probes the question "How does a person come into right relationship with God?" It is pivotal in the unfolding of Christian history. Fifteen hundred years after Paul wrote this letter, a German monk named Martin Luther found it to be his guide out of bondage into Christian freedom. He wrote of it, "The Epistle to the Galatians is my epistle; I have betrothed myself to it: it is my wife." [1] It is pertinent for today, for Christianity is still threatened by legalistic cults and self-righteous pride. A close look at the letter in its original setting will help us to understand its message and apply its truth to our lives.

The Author

Except for one or two extreme critics of an earlier period, no one questions that Paul the apostle was the author of Galatians. Not only did he give us his name at the beginning (1:1) and near the end (5:2); he devoted the first two chapters to describing his experience as the missionary to the Gentiles. No one but Paul fits the description given there. He was a dedicated leader of the Jews who persecuted Christians (1:13-14). He was converted and called to preach to the Gentiles in a dramatic series of events at Damascus (1:15-17). After three years he visited Jerusalem where he saw Cephas (Peter) and James, the brother of Jesus (1:18-20). After this he spent a long period in Syria and Cilicia, the area of Asia Minor which included Paul's hometown of Tarsus (1:21-24). Then, fourteen years later, he made another visit to Jerusalem, taking Barnabas and Titus with him (2:1). On this occasion the Jerusalem church leaders recognized his mission to the Gentiles (2:2-10). He was a leader in the church at Antioch, speaking with authority even to Barnabas and Cephas over the question of fellowship with the Gentiles (2:11-14).

Some important characteristics of the apostle shine through the letter. He was a preacher who stated his theology against a background of intense personal experience. He received his message by revelation (1:12)—that is, by direct contact with Jesus Christ. He was independent of all controlling influences except Christ. He wrote with passion and power. Deeply spiritual, he was also thoroughly human. He expressed surprise (1:6), disappointment, and fear (4:11). He was perplexed (4:20). He showed anger and impatience (1:9; 2:14; 5:12; 6:17).

The Readers

Paul addressed his letter "to the churches of Galatia" (1:2) and called the readers "Galatians" (3:1). Where is Galatia, and who are the Galatians? There are two possible answers to this question and much disagreement as to which is correct.

First of all, Galatia was a mountainous territory in central Asia Minor (modern-day Turkey). It included the cities of Pessinus, Ancyra (Ankara, the capital of Turkey today), and Tavium. In the third century B.C. wandering tribes of Gauls from Europe entered the area. They fought with the inhabitants until they were overcome and confined to the region which came to be known as the kingdom of Galatia, after the name "Gaul." Galatia continued to be an independent kingdom until the death of King Amyntas in 25 B.C. At this time the area came under Roman control.

The Romans expanded the province of Galatia southward to include parts of Lycaonia, Phrygia, and Pisidia. Thus the name Galatia could mean the old kingdom in the northern highlands or the Roman province which included other territory in the south.

Throughout much of Christian history it was thought that Paul addressed his letter to territorial or ethnic Galatia, the area of the old Gallic kingdom. This view is called the North Galatian theory. It assumes that Paul did missionary work in North Galatia (Acts 16:6) on his second missionary journey and at the beginning of the third journey (Acts 18:23). Some commentators, mostly European scholars, continue to hold this view today.

Other commentators, including most British and American scholars, prefer the South Galatian theory, although they admit there are some good arguments on both sides. In this view, Galatia refers to the Roman

province, particularly the southern part where Paul on his first missionary journey founded churches at Antioch of Pisidia, Iconium, Lystra, and Derbe.

Advocates of the North Galatian theory point out that in the book
of Acts Luke did not speak of Antioch, Lystra, Derbe, and Iconium
as towns of Galatia; so Paul would not likely do so. They assert that
Galatia must be a geographical term because Luke used geographical
designations such as Pisidia, Phrygia, and Lycaonia in Acts. Furthermore, they say, the people of the southern area would not be called
Galatians even when their province was called Galatia.

Proponents of the South Galatian theory say that in his other writings Paul spoke in terms of Roman provinces, not geographical territories. They also feel that the isolated, mountainous area of North Galatia
would not likely be the scene of activity by the Judaizers who worked
against Paul. Paul spoke of Barnabas as one well known to the Galatians, and we know that Barnabas accompanied Paul on his campaign
in the southern territory. Finally, they contend, there is no clear evidence that Paul was ever in the territory of North Galatia. It is more
reasonable, they say, to think in terms of the area where we have
abundant records of Paul's activity.

The evidence for the South Galatian theory seems more convincing,
although not irrefutable. In either case, the interpretation of the letter
is not changed. The major point of difference would be in the dating.

Date

The North Galatian theory would require a later date for the writing,
since the supposed work in that area began later than in the south.
Those who hold that view date the writing during the third missionary
journey, possibly from Ephesus around A.D. 55.

The South Galatian view permits, but does not require, an earlier
date. Some scholars believe it was written before the Jerusalem conference described in Acts 15 because it does not mention that momentous
decision regarding ministry to the Gentiles. If it were written before
that council, it would be dated around A.D. 49 and would be the
earliest of Paul's letters. This early date would make it easier to understand Peter's inconsistent attitude toward fellowship with Gentiles
(Gal. 2:11-14).

Others believe that the theology expressed in Galatians is closer
to that found in Romans and 1 and 2 Corinthians, which were written

later. They maintain that an earlier writing would reflect more of the doctrinal concerns seen in 1 and 2 Thessalonians, which were written earlier. They, whether North or South Galatianists, date the letter around A.D. 55. Research for this present volume, having included a study of 2 Corinthians, makes the later date seem more natural, so it will be assumed for this discussion. In either case, the dating does not affect the interpretation.

Occasion and Purpose

It is very easy for Christians today to forget that the first believers were Jews. They continued to be Jews after they became Christians. At first it did not dawn on them that one could be a Christian and not be a Jew. Only gradually did they come to appreciate that the gospel provided a radically new and different basis for right relationship with God. It was hard for them to conceive of a man who was in right standing with God but was not circumcised and did not keep the requirements of the Jewish law. Paul had been as devoted to the law and the traditions of Judaism as anyone, but he was the first to see fully and clearly that these things were not necessary. God led him to preach salvation to the Gentiles, and he quickly saw that faith in Christ, not works of the law, made a man righteous.

There were other Christians besides Paul who had been Pharisees. When Paul and Barnabas returned from the first missionary journey, they found some of these at Antioch telling the believers that circumcision was essential for salvation (Acts 15:1). This led to a conference at Jerusalem where again converted Pharisees urged obedience to the law of Moses (Acts 15:5). The council, under the leadership of James and Peter, decreed that Gentile believers were not to be burdened with the Jewish law. Their letter to this effect indicated that the Judaizers had already been active not only at Antioch, but throughout Syria and in Cilicia (Acts 15:23-24).

With this background in mind, it is easy to understand what must have happened in the Galatian churches. Paul had come to Galatia with the good news of salvation in Christ. Most of those who believed were Gentiles. They had no background in Judaism. They found salvation and freedom in Christ. But when Paul left the area his opponents, the Judaizers, were not far behind. Soon the Galatian believers were led astray (Gal. 1:6). Like most new converts, they were eager to do right and to prove their faithfulness. When these new teachers

came, claiming the authority of the Jerusalem apostles, their appeal
was irresistible. The new Christians were ready to add circumcision
and the law to their faith in Christ.

To Paul, this was a most serious crisis. If this were allowed to go
unchecked, Christianity would lapse into being a cult of Judaism. Freedom in Christ would be exchanged for a new kind of slavery. The
gospel would be hopelessly distorted. Strong, decisive action was called
for. The apostle sat down and, under the leadership of the Holy Spirit,
wrote an impassioned restatement of the gospel of grace.

Contents and Style

The message of Galatians can be summed up in one key verse:
"For freedom Christ has set us free; stand fast therefore, and do not
submit again to a yoke of slavery" (5:1).

The book is composed of three sections of two chapters each. Chapters 1—2 give Paul's personal history as the basis for his appeal to
the Galatians. Chapters 3—4 give his theological appeal. Chapters
5—6 give his challenge to spiritual living.

The argument is strong and thorough. Paul detailed the history
of his apostleship to counter the false claims of the Judaizers (1:1 to
2:14). He developed his doctrine of salvation by grace from many
angles, beginning with his own personal testimony (2:15-21). He then
appealed to the Galatians' own experience (3:1-5). Next he turned
to the Old Testament, showing Abraham to be the prototype of justification by faith (3:6-18). He went on to discuss law and promise, showing that the role of the law is temporary, while faith in God's word
is permanent (3:19-29). He warned against returning to bondage and
reminded them of his experience with them (4:8-20). He climaxed
this doctrinal section with an allegory drawn from the story of Abraham, illustrating spiritual truth with historical events, an approach
much used in the ancient world (4:21-31). On this basis, he made
his practical appeal (chaps. 5—6).

The style of the letter is interesting and impressive. Paul used many
colorful figures of speech. There are numerous rhetorical questions.
Personal references give the letter warmth. By using the first person
plural "we," Paul identified himself with his readers. Although we
do not know the effect of the letter in Galatia, the fact that it was
preserved and treasured in the churches would indicate that it was

effective in its mission. Paul's skill as a communicator is evident throughout.

Meaning for Today

At first glance Galatians seems to be an argument against circumcision and other requirements of Jewish legalism. If that is all we see, it will not seem very meaningful for contemporary life. Those issues were settled long ago. The key to reading Galatians in the present tense is to see the larger, basic issues.

Galatians is really a book about the relationship between persons and God. How can a man or woman find peace with God and live in harmony with him? The answer is "through faith in Jesus Christ." The problem comes when we try to add other requirements. There is a strong tendency for people to add other requirements or to substitute them for faith in Christ altogether. Although circumcision may not be an issue today, other things are. It is significant that every cult and distorted form of religion that becomes popular involves some kind of legalism. Other things are added as requirements for salvation. And even within the major Christian churches, there is always the danger that we will substitute our own requirements for God's way of redemption. Why is legalism such a persistent danger?

For one thing, legalism appeals to pride, while faith in Christ requires repentance and humility. As long as religion can be reduced to regulations, those who try hard can feel good about their accomplishments. To say "My only hope is the grace of God in Christ" is hard on the ego.

Legalism is also more natural to human experience. It puts religion on the same basis as most of the rest of our experiences which are transactions involving effort and competition.

Legalism is also easier to manage than grace. If righteousness can be reduced to certain well-defined duties, a person can do these more easily than he can exercise a life-changing faith. Christian freedom requires the inner motivation of the Holy Spirit, but legalism provides the external force of laws and punishments. Those who administer the regulations can control other people, as so many cult leaders do, by defining the rules their way.

Finally, legalism seems safer than grace. Freedom is dangerous. If matters are left up to the conscience of the individual, there is more danger of confusion and mistakes. Insecure people fear that life will get out of control, and they feel better if someone with authority will tell them what to do.

Galatians not only speaks to the endless danger of legalism; it also speaks to another trend in modern life, the abuse of freedom and the absence of moral order. The legalists are right in that control is needed. They are wrong about where the control must come from. Outward restrictions of the law are mostly ineffective in creating moral living. Such morality can only come from within as persons are energized by the Spirit of God.

Paul was aware of the danger that people would use freedom as an excuse to do what they wanted to do. This he saw would become another kind of slavery in itself. The answer to this need for control is not man-made regulations; it is acceptance of Christ as Lord and the Holy Spirit as helper. A. M. Hunter has summarized it well by saying, "The Judaizers said: 'Do these things, and live.' The Christian says, 'Live, and do these things.' " [2]

Personal Appeal

1:1 to 2:21

Greetings (1:1-5)

Paul began his letters with the standard form for letters of that day. The writer named himself and then his readers, expressed a greeting to them, and included some wish or prayer for them. But Paul's letters were more than ordinary letters. They were inspired statements of the gospel and impassioned defenses of his mission. Even in the greeting of each letter he stated his deepest convictions and outlined key points in his message. This is especially true in these first verses of Galatians. In each of Paul's letters the greeting is different at certain points. Here in Galatians he omitted his usual words of encouragement and appreciation. Serious business took priority, and he wanted his readers to know that he was disappointed in them.

In identifying himself, Paul came quickly to one of the major issues.

The Judaizers who had come to Galatia had questioned his authority as an apostle, so he added an important phrase to his usual "Paul an apostle." Our word apostle is the very word Paul used in Greek, carried over into English. Its basic meaning is "one who is sent." It identifies Paul as God's specially appointed messenger. The word was originally applied to the twelve whom Jesus chose to be his primary witnesses. When the eleven sought a replacement for Judas, they specified that an apostle should be one who had been present throughout the earthly ministry of Jesus and most particularly one who was a witness of the resurrected Lord (Acts 1:21-22). But Paul knew that Christ himself had called him to be an apostle. He had not been with the others during the ministry of Jesus, but he had met the risen Lord on the Damascus road. There was no doubt in his mind that he was an apostle too.

Paul added another pair of phrases to his usual identification. His credentials did not depend on any human authority. His apostleship did not come "from men"—that is, from the other apostles, or "through man," by way of Ananias or any human intermediary. His authority was the one who called him, Jesus Christ. He recognized that when Christ commissioned him, God the Father did too.

Paul further identified God as the one "who raised him from the dead." This is significant because it was the risen Lord who called Paul and made him an apostle. But Paul was thinking of more than his own apostleship here. He was pointing to the basis of the gospel itself. Throughout Galatians Paul pointed to Jesus Christ as the one who made persons right with God. Paul's hope of life depended on the fact that Christ died and was alive so that those who die to sin with him can live as he lives in them (Gal. 2:20).

Paul frequently included his traveling companions in his correspondence and usually named them. Here he simply said, "And all the brethren who are with me." He either assumed that the Galatians knew who was with him or he was too occupied with the urgent matter before him to concern himself with listing the names. He did identify his readers as "the churches of Galatia." This probably refers to the Roman province of Galatia in Asia Minor and includes the congregations at Derbe, Lystra, Iconium, and Antioch of Pisidia. As was mentioned in the Introduction, some scholars believe that Paul was referring to unnamed congregations in the old territory of Galatia to the north.

At this point in a letter, writers of Paul's day included a common word meaning "greetings." Paul always used a slightly different form of the word which means "grace." This is one of the great Christian words, indicating all of that undeserved goodness which God gives to his people in saving and sustaining them. It is especially appropriate here in Galatians, where the problem is a failure to understand grace.

To his basic greeting Paul added another which was well known to the Oriental world. "Peace" (even today the Hebrew greeting *Shalom* is recognized by many people) was both an ancient greeting and a good word to sum up the blessings of Christ. Taken together, grace and peace sum up Christianity by pointing to what God does and what persons experience in Christ. These blessings come from God the Father and our Lord Jesus Christ. They are not products of human effort.

To emphasize further that Christ, not the law, is the source of salvation, Paul said more about the work of Christ. He gave himself for our sins. The answer to the problem of sin is the death of Christ on the cross, not obedience to legal requirements. Only by his accomplishment can we be free of the present evil age. Sin is not just a problem of adjustment within a person which he can overcome by a legal transaction. It is a whole way of life and system of society which can only be overcome by a new system and a new way. The gospel says that the old age, the sinful world order, has been broken by Christ and the new age of the kingdom of God has begun.

All of this, Paul noted, has happened according to the will of God. The death of Christ was not an accident or the product of human scheming. It was what God planned and intended. This thought led Paul to break out in an expression of praise. His feeling was intense as he thought of the great salvation offered by Christ in contrast to the poor substitute being considered by the Galatians.

No Other Gospel (1:6-10)

Paul usually began his letters with words of appreciation for his readers. For the Galatians, however, he had only strong words of disappointment. He wanted them to know how shocked he was at the new turn they had taken, as if his astonishment would startle them into awareness. He also let them know in no uncertain terms that the course they had taken was wrong. He contrasted the message of the Judaizers with the gospel. It seemed to be another gospel, but it was so different that it was not a gospel at all. The Greek text has two words for "another." The Revised Standard Version translates the first one with "different."

In turning from the gospel to legalism, they had deserted the one who called them, God himself. The term "deserted" is a striking word which is used of a change of attitude or even a military revolt. The grace of Christ was their rightful allegiance, and they had abandoned this.

Having spoken of a different gospel in verse 6, Paul guarded his meaning in verse 7. He wanted to be sure they understood that there could be no other gospel. Any different message was no gospel at all. "Gospel" is the English equivalent of a Greek word meaning good news. The only good news concerning salvation from sin is the revelation of God's grace in the death and resurrection of Jesus Christ and the possibility of new life through faith in him. To add the requirements of the law to this would not be good news at all, and it would say that the work of Christ was inadequate, thereby canceling the good news. So Paul said the preachers of this non-gospel were perverting the gospel of Christ. He singled them out and let the Galatians know he was aware of what was going on when he said, "There are some who trouble you." These Judaizers were saying, "Faith in Christ is not enough. You must also be circumcised and obey the law of the old covenant."

Paul now indicated that there was more involved than which teacher one listened to. It didn't matter who brought the message; the question was whether that message was the gospel of Christ. To make this clear, Paul said that even if an angel or he himself should show up with a different message, the messenger should be rejected. There was only one gospel, and they had received that when Paul first preached to them.

The apostle used very harsh language here, for he said that the false messenger should be "accursed." His actual word was a Greek term that has been carried over into English, "anathema." It was used to translate a Hebrew word meaning devoted to God for destruction. It denotes something which is totally rejected by God; like idols and valuable goods which the Israelites captured in battle with their enemies and which they were commanded to destroy. Paul felt that the offense of the Judaizers was so serious that drastic action should be taken. He had given this warning before and was repeating something they should know already.

Such language does not sound like a man who would do anything

to have people like him. But that was what his enemies said about
him. They apparently told the Galatians that Paul left out the requirement of the law to make his gospel more acceptable. In verse 10
he countered that charge. It was God's favor he sought, and he was
a servant of Christ. It should be clear at this point that he was no
compromiser for the sake of popularity.

God's Revelation to Paul (1:11-17)

Having stated the problem, Paul now began to develop his argument. He began with an attention-getting phrase, "I would have you
know," to stress the importance of what he was about to say. He
addressed the Galatians as brethren, as he did eight other times in
the letter, to assure them that he and they were still united in Christ
even though there was a serious issue between them.

The first line of argument is personal history. It had been claimed
that Paul was not an authoritative source for understanding the gospel
because he received his message from others, principally the Jerusalem apostles. Thus he had no right to say what was the true gospel.
Paul insisted that his message is not "man's gospel," literally "not
according to man" (The New English Bible says, "no human inven-
tion"). He did not receive it from some other human, either Ananias,
the Antioch church, or the apostles. It was not some teaching based
on Judaism or philosophical systems.

The source of his gospel, Paul insisted, is "a revelation of Jesus
Christ." Obviously he was thinking of his conversion experience on
the road to Damascus. Paul knew some of the facts about Jesus before
this, but he did not understand them. He surely learned more from
others along the way. But his personal relationship with Christ and
his understanding of the gospel came when the living Lord appeared
to him and accepted him in sheer grace. This could not be explained
away by any human factor. On the contrary, the human factors all
pointed the other way.

The Galatians were aware of Paul's preconversion life. No doubt
he had referred to it often in giving his testimony. His roots were
in Judaism, giving him excellent credentials to refute the Judaizers.
So intense was his commitment to Judaism that he persecuted the
church and tried to destroy it. Not only was he the equal of other
Jews; he was at the head of his class. He outdid his peers in his zeal.
He was totally committed to upholding the teachings of his ancestors.

Paul said this to make two points. First, his background did not explain his conversion. For such a Jewish leader to change would require divine intervention. His changed life was proof of the validity of his experience. Secondly, he knew what he was talking about when he discussed the law. No one could accuse him of not understanding the subject at hand.

Verse 15 is a beautiful description of the change that had taken place and a profound explanation of it. Paul was convinced that God had his eye on him all along. Before he was born, God had plans for his life. Because of his grace, and not any merit in Paul, God had called him to salvation and service. Thus God revealed his Son to Paul (literally "in me"). Paul's encounter with Christ resulted in a relationship of union with Christ so that Paul could preach Christ to the Gentiles. Not only his words, but his very life became the instrument of showing Christ to others.

Even after this, Paul did not immediately turn to human sources for direction. He did not even call upon the apostles in Jerusalem to get guidance or approval. Instead, he went into Arabia. We do not know exactly where. The term was loosely applied to a large area in which Arab people lived, including the area around Damascus and extending southward to include such areas as Sinai. Nor do we know how long he stayed. It was less than three years, for during that span he preached at Damascus before visiting Jerusalem (v. 18). We do not even know why he went or what he did in Arabia. Presumably it was not to preach, for his preaching strategy was always to go to more populous areas. Most likely he went to pray and meditate. Like Moses, Elijah, and Jesus, he used a time of solitude to prepare for a life of activity. Following this he returned to Damascus, preached there, and went on to Jerusalem (Acts 9:19-29).

Paul's First Visit to Jerusalem (1:18-24)

Three years passed. By Jewish reckoning this could have been part of one year, a full year in between, and part of a third year. The time was probably marked from Paul's conversion, but it could have been from his return to Damascus. Only after this time lapse did Paul go to Jerusalem. This was evidence that he was completely independent of the influence of the apostles.

He went to get to know Cephas (the Aramaic name for Peter). The word translated "to visit" is used of travelers who visit a person or place to get acquainted. Thus Paul did not go to be instructed by Peter. This visit lasted fifteen days, long enough for Paul to fill out his knowledge of the life and ministry of Jesus and to confirm that he and Peter shared the same gospel. Having accomplished this purpose, Paul did not become further involved with the other apostles. He did, however, meet James, the brother of Jesus, whom he included as an apostle even though he was not one of the twelve. The term apostle was apparently extended to other leaders beyond the original circle. James, although not a believer in Jesus before the Lord's death, was a witness of the resurrection (1 Cor. 15:7); and he became one of the leaders of the Jerusalem church, according to the book of Acts.

In verse 20 Paul inserted a solemn assertion that what he was saying was the truth. This is hard to understand unless his opponents had given some other account of the matter. The issue was so important that Paul felt he must set the record straight in the clearest possible terms. He was not a secondary apostle, dependent on others for his message and subject to their correction. His faith and his calling came by revelation from Christ himself.

Paul left Jerusalem, according to Acts 9:29-30, because his preaching aroused the anger of the Greek-speaking Jews in Jerusalem. His life in danger, he was sent off to Tarsus. He referred here to the regions of Syria and Cilicia, neighboring territories which were part of the same Roman province. Antioch was the chief city of Syria; and Tarsus, Paul's home city, was the major city of Cilicia. He remained unknown in the churches of Judea, where he would likely have worked if he had been under the direction of the apostles in Jerusalem. The Judean Christians did, however, hear about Paul. The change in him was widely reported. He had gone from persecutor to preacher. There was no note of bragging when Paul said, "They glorified God because of me." He himself gave the credit to God and was glad that others did too. Thus Paul was a true convert to Christ and a recognized missionary. He was well thought of by the Christians in Jerusalem, but he was in no way dependent on them. He was an apostle in his own right.

Paul's Second Visit to Jerusalem (2:1-10)

Paul had established the fact that he was independent of the leaders at Jerusalem. Now he proceeded to show that they approved his gospel and his mission to the Gentiles without asking him to require circumcision. Fourteen years passed. It is not clear whether Paul was counting from his conversion or from his first visit to Jerusalem. The latter seems a more natural interpretation of the word "then," immediately following the account of the first visit.

It is also impossible to tell whether this second visit to Jerusalem was the same as the visit in Acts 11:27-30, when the Antioch church sent Paul with relief during a famine, or whether the visit of Acts 15 was meant, when Paul and the Jerusalem apostles settled the question of the mission to the Gentiles in a formal council. There are good arguments for both interpretations, and the meaning of Galatians is the same in either case. If Paul meant the council visit, then he was leaving out the famine visit in a passage where sequence of events was important. On the other hand, the essential features of the visit sound more like the council visit. In either view, a long time passed during which Paul had no contact with the Jerusalem church.

Paul took Barnabas and Titus with him. Although Paul was not well known to the Judean Christians, Barnabas was. He had been sent from Jerusalem to investigate and assist the work in Antioch, and he had been involved in the mission to the Gentiles from the very beginning (Acts 11:22-26; 13:2-3). He was thus a key link in the relationship between Jewish and Gentile Christians. Titus was not known in Jerusalem, but he served to represent the Gentiles converted under Paul's ministry. The question of whether he should be circumcised became the focus of controversy on this occasion.

Paul did not go because of his own desire to consult with Jerusalem. Nor did they send for him. He went as the result of a revelation from God. Only because he felt divine leadership did he initiate further consultation with the other apostles, again evidence that he was God's apostle, not Jerusalem's.

In a private meeting with the recognized leaders, Paul outlined his gospel message. In verse 9 these leaders are identified as James, Cephas, and John. The phrase "those who were of repute" may be a term Paul's critics had used to support their appeal to the apostles. He made this presentation, he said, "Lest somehow I should be running or had run in vain." From Paul's other statements we can be sure that he did not have any doubts about the truth of the gospel as he preached it. Rather, he felt a need to be in harmony with the other apostles and to have them understand that they shared the one and only gospel in unity. Christian unity was important to Paul (Gal. 3:28). He felt that his mission would be seriously injured if others did not recognize that they were all engaged in the same great enterprise.

Verses 3-5 are not clear. There are breaks in the sentence structure apparently caused by the great emotion under which Paul was writing. There are also a few lesser manuscripts which leave out the word "not" in verse 5, making it seem that Paul gave in and had Titus circumcised. Although some commentators take this view, the majority follow the better manuscripts and a more reasonable view of Paul's stand and maintain that Titus was not circumcised.

Verse 3 is the first mention of circumcision in the epistle. It is easy to see why the question of circumcision arose with regard to Titus. Here, in Jerusalem itself, Paul introduced a Gentile as a brother in Christ. Jewish Christians were faced with the issue person to person. Circumcision is a minor medical matter today, the surgical removal of a fold of flesh called the foreskin from the penis. It is done routinely when male children are born where advanced medical techniques are followed, regardless of religious affiliation. For the ancient Hebrews, however, it was a sign of the covenant relationship with God dating back to Abraham (Gen. 17:10-14). It was commanded by God himself, and anyone not circumcised could not be a member of God's chosen people. Under Moses it became a requirement of the law (Ex. 12:43-48). No wonder Jews who were Christians had doubts about Christians who were not circumcised.

Paul emphasized that Titus was not compelled to be circumcised on this occasion. The Jerusalem apostles did not require this, even though there were agitators present who tried to force the issue. Their aim, Paul said, was to undermine the freedom which we have in Christ, a step which would result in bondage. Paul stood firm in order to preserve the gospel for the sake of his brethren on the Gentile mission field. Those who demanded circumcision of the Galatians were asking for something which had not been required by the apostles at Jerusalem.

The reputation of the apostles had already been referred to in verse 2. Now, in verse 6, Paul rejected the idea that there is any rank or authority that determines spiritual truth. God shows no partiality toward men of reputation, and Paul did not either. It was, however, significant to Paul that those recognized leaders did not add anything to his gospel. Therefore, the Judaizers in Galatia had no grounds for doing so.

What the other apostles did do was to recognize that Paul had been given the true gospel and a commission to preach it to the Gentiles. He and Peter had parallel ministries. Here Paul used the Greek name Peter because this was the name by which Simon Peter was recognized as an apostle by the Greek-speaking world. Elsewhere he used the Aramaic *Cephas* by which Simon Peter was personally known and addressed. Peter, and the others whom he represented, had been given the gospel and the opportunity to preach it to the Jews. This does not mean that there was a strict division or limit, for Paul also preached to Jews; and Peter preached to Gentiles on occasion. There was simply a general working arrangement. Verse 8 is crucial. It was God working in both cases who validated the ministry of these men. The word "mission" is literally "apostleship." Thus Paul was clearly putting his role as an apostle on an equal basis with Peter's.

It was obvious to the apostles that Paul had received the grace of God. They shook hands to symbolize their agreement. Thus James and Cephas and John gave unmistakable recognition to Paul's gospel and his mission to the Gentiles. They made just one special request, that Paul should remember the poor, the Christians in Jerusalem who were suffering persecution and loss of property. Paul was already doing this, having brought an offering for the poor from Antioch, either on this visit or an earlier one. He was eager to continue this, both to meet a pressing need and to cement the bond of friendship between Jewish and Gentile Christians. Throughout his ministry he gave much attention to such relief work (1 Cor. 16:1-4; 2 Cor. 8-9; Rom. 15:25-29).

Confrontation with Peter (2:11-14)

Paul's visit to Jerusalem did not settle the relations of Jews and Gentiles in the church. That was made terribly clear when Peter paid a visit to Antioch. There he found Jews and Gentiles enjoying unbroken fellowship, including a common meal. This was a revolutionary thing, for Jews simply did not eat with Gentiles. The law did not specifically forbid it, but it did impose restrictions on diet which would exclude Jews from a Gentile table. And developments in Jewish history had caused them to take extreme measures to avoid contaminating their way of life with Gentile contacts.

The agreement worked out earlier at Jerusalem said that Gentiles did not have to assume the burden of the Jewish law. It did not say that Jews could be free of it. It approved sending missionaries to the Gentiles, but it said nothing about close fellowship with them. Peter accepted the open fellowship of the congregation at Antioch and joined in.

But other Jewish believers were also interested in what was going on at Antioch. James himself did not come, but some of his associates did. Their presence, and perhaps their reaction, caused Peter to fear the circumcision party. He withdrew from the group meals. Worse, the other Jews joined him. The term translated "acted insincerely" is literally "played the hypocrite." Even Barnabas was swept along by their hypocritical behavior.

This must have been a severe blow to the fellowship at Antioch. Paul acted quickly and decisively. He confronted Peter in the presence of the whole congregation because the whole congregation was involved in what he was doing; and the principle was vital for all concerned. He pointed out Peter's inconsistency. He was formally holding to the Jewish law, but he was actually living much like the Gentiles. It was wrong for him, then, to expect Gentiles to live up to a way of life which he did not support by his own behavior.

No Justification Through the Law (2:15-21)

The Greek text does not have quotation marks, and it is not clear just where Paul's words to Peter leave off and where he resumed his argument to the Galatians. The Revised Standard Version ends the quote after verse 14, and the passage that follows does seem to be more general, although it is in direct reference to Peter's offense. Paul began as though he were talking about Peter and himself, "we who are Jews," in contrast to those the Judaizers called "Gentile sinners." Peter, like Paul, had learned that there was no salvation for him in Jewish legal observance. Both had experienced justification through their faith in Christ. Justification is a legal term Paul used frequently to describe salvation. It means acquittal, being set right with God or being reckoned righteous. Even though they were Jews, they had found a right relationship with God only through faith in Christ. No one, Paul said, not even the most faithful Jew, could be justified by the works of the law. "Works of the law" seems to include any religious system by which people think they can earn God's approval by their own accomplishments.

Verse 17 is difficult to interpret. It may mean that justification by faith in Christ shows Jews like Paul and Peter to be sinners just like the Gentiles. This then could raise the objection that Christ is an agent of sin because he brought them to such a situation. Such a conclusion is unthinkable to Paul. The phrase "Certainly not!" is a strong one, almost an oath, that literally says, "Let it not be so!"

It is not Christ who causes people to be sinners. In verse 18 Paul pointed the finger of blame at those who try to establish their legal righteousness, as Peter did, by going back to the law after they had already recognized the futility of the law. Such a person proved that he was a transgressor, one who violated the law.

Paul now moved to a personal testimony of his experience. As he thought of Christians such as the Judaizers who tried to go back to the law as the way of righteousness, he was struck by the impossibility of it. He had tried that way once, but his efforts only resulted in death. He was dead to the law in that he no longer lived a life that was controlled by the law. And he was dead to the law in the sense that he no longer held any hope that the law could lead to life. This death to the law opened up the possibility that he could now live "to God"—that is, live a life in which God is the controlling force and God supplies life.

The change from law to grace came through Paul's relationship with Christ, specifically Christ's death. Paul had died to his old life just as Christ had died on the cross. The person who now lived and wrote was not that old, legalistic Saul of Tarsus. He was a new person filled and controlled by Christ. Christ lived in Paul, a mystery that cannot be explained but can be experienced by all who come into personal union with Christ by faith. This does not mean that Paul had no separate identity, for he went on to say "the life I now live in the flesh, I live" (v. 20). Being crucified with Christ does not wipe out the believer's individual identity; it sets him free to be his true, best self. That authentic self is the person God meant him to be, a person "conformed to the image of his Son" (Rom. 8:29).

This new life in union with Christ can be lived only by faith, a deep personal commitment to Christ. It is possible because Christ took the initiative in love and gave himself for every person. To try

to live it any other way—by obedience to the law, for example—
would do away with the grace of God. Paul said that if a person
could be right with God through the law, Christ's death would be
unnecessary. The death of Christ is eloquent evidence that no lesser
solution is adequate. Nothing less than his death could save. Nothing
more than his death is necessary. Paul's statement that he did not
"nullify the grace of God" implied that the Judaizers did.

Biblical and Theological Appeal

3:1 to 4:31

Probing Questions (3:1-5)

In chapters 3 and 4 Paul turned from the evidence of his personal
experience to evidence based on theology. But the transition in verses
1-5 was based on an appeal to the experience of the Galatian Christians. Paul asked them a question which showed his astonishment
at their deviation and directed their attention to its unreasonableness.
He addressed them as "foolish Galatians," implying that they were
failing to use their mental ability. Someone must have bewitched
them, a term that described a sorcerer casting a spell or "evil eye."
If they had not been so hypnotized, they could see the truth in Christ.
Paul had publicly portrayed Christ and his crucifixion before them.
The term he used here could be translated literally as "placarded."
In ancient times news was made public by means of a placard
set up in some public place. In such a way, Paul said, the gospel of
Christ had been as plainly set before them as a billboard. If they had
missed it, the only explanation must be that they had been under a
spell.

The dramatic question of verse 1 is followed by four rhetorical
questions. Paul was not asking for an answer; he was stating a fact
and drawing attention to it by means of a question. The first point
he made was that the Galatians did not come to experience life in
the Spirit by doing works of the law, but by hearing the gospel and

receiving it with faith. Here Paul described the Christian life in terms
of receiving the Spirit instead of being justified. Justification is God's
activity in salvation; receiving the Spirit is man's experience. Paul
was here focusing on the experience of his Galatian friends. He would
return to the contrast between law and Spirit in chapter 5. The question, then, was why should the Galatians go back to the law, when
it was hearing and faith that brought the life of God into their lives?

Next Paul raised the contrast between Spirit and flesh, a basic concept in the latter part of the book. How foolish and tragic to start
out with the Spirit, the presence of God in a person's life, and to go
from there to the flesh, human nature as it was apart from God.

Paul went on to question whether the Galatians had learned anything from their experience. "Did you experience?" could be translated "Did you suffer?" The word can mean either experience in a
neutral sense or bad experience, usually the latter in the New Testament. Whichever Paul meant here, the point was, "Did you learn
anything from it, or has it been wasted?" Paul was not sure that it
was in vain, so he added a statement to that effect after the question.

The fourth and final rhetorical question concerned the wonderful
things God had done in their lives. He had given his Spirit. Miracles
had happened. "Do you really think," Paul asked, "that those things
happened because of your law-keeping? No, they came about because
you responded in faith to the gospel you heard."

The Example of Abraham (3:6-9)

Paul now turned from experience to Scripture as the basis of his
argument. The point he had been making, that salvation comes
through faith and not through law, was proved by Abraham. The
Judaizers had surely spoken to the Galatians about Abraham. He was
the father of the Jewish people, and circumcision began with him
(Gen. 17:10-14). But Paul pointed to Genesis 15:6 to show that Abraham's righteousness came as he accepted God's promise by faith. Before Abraham was circumcised, and long before the law was given
to Moses, Abraham was righteous in the sight of God simply by faith
in God's promise. In Romans 4:11-12, Paul went on to explain the
significance of circumcision: "He received circumcision as a sign or
seal of the righteousness which he had by faith while he was still
uncircumcised. The purpose was to make him the father of all who

believe without being circumcised and who thus have righteousness reckoned to them, and likewise the father of the circumcised who are not merely circumcised but also follow the example of the faith which our father Abraham had before he was circumcised."

It was not circumcision, then, but faith that made persons children of Abraham. When Abraham received God's promise and believed, Paul said he was receiving the gospel. He didn't know all we know about Christ, but he believed the promise of blessing that was later fulfilled in Christ. Paul was saying that there has never been any way of salvation other than accepting by faith the promise of God and receiving the righteousness which God alone can give. Anyone who will do as he did will receive the same blessing.

The Curse of the Law (3:10-14)

Not only does the law not bring blessing; it actually imposes a curse. Paul cited Deuteronomy 27:26, which says that anyone who does not keep the law is cursed. Paul knew that no one could keep all of the law; therefore, all were under this curse. Furthermore, he maintained that keeping the law was never intended to be the way to be right with God. Quoting Habakkuk 2:4, he said, "He who through faith is righteous shall live." At this point the King James Version probably gives the more natural sense of the words, taking "by faith" with "live" instead of "righteous." "The just shall live by his faith." The original statement in Habakkuk uses faith in the sense of faithfulness, but the idea of trusting God is still present.

The way of law is completely different from the way of faith. Quoting Leviticus 18:5, Paul pointed out that the law requires doing, not trusting. The law dealt with actions. Only if one could do what the law required could he hope to gain life that way. Thus the law and the hopeless burden of trying to keep the law were seen to be a curse.

Everything is different for those who trust in Christ. He has redeemed believers from the curse of the law. The word translated "redeemed" means to buy back or to ransom. It was used to describe the purchase of slaves. He did this by becoming a curse for us. Paul quoted Deuteronomy 21:23, which prohibited hanging the body of an executed criminal on a tree. It was felt that the condemned man was under a curse, and to leave his body publicly displayed would bring a curse on the land; therefore, he was to be buried and not left in the open. Christ, then, became our substitute and representa-

tive, taking on himself the curse of the law. In doing this he broke
or exhausted the curse and provided the needed alternative. Now
in Christ, the blessing God spoke of to Abraham can come to the
Gentiles. Anyone who will put his faith in Christ can receive the
Spirit, the experience of God in his life which comes by being in
right relationship with God.

The Promised Inheritance (3:15-18)

Paul illustrated his argument by giving an example from common
experience. He spoke of the making of a "will," according to the
Revised Standard Version, but the word is the same one translated
"covenant" in verse 17. While the ordinary Greek usage would probably refer to a will, the biblical usage would be covenant. Probably
Paul meant here any kind of a contract or formal agreement, such
as an exchange of property. The point was that such a contract was
binding and was not changed except by the party who made it.

Paul interrupted his thought to indicate that he was thinking of
the covenant God made with Abraham in Genesis 13:15 and 17:7-8.
This covenant was not just with Abraham; it was also promised to
his "offspring," literally "seed." Paul found profound significance in
the fact that a singular word was used of this offspring. Of course
he knew that the singular could be collective and included all the
members of Abraham's descendants. But the grammatical point reminded him of what he already knew from other sources. Christ was
Abraham's descendant, and Christ was the head of the new humanity
God was creating. As such he included in himself all who are Abraham's spiritual descendants. He was not proving this truth from the
Old Testament; he was illustrating it. Such reasoning was commonly
used and accepted by the religious teachers of Paul's day. In Paul's
mind, this meant that the covenant with Abraham was not over and
done with in Abraham's day. It was intended to continue into the
life of Christ and his people.

The Judaizers would have said that the giving of the law to Moses
took priority over God's dealing with Abraham. Paul pointed out that
the law came 430 years after Abraham. This was the length of Israel's
stay in Egypt, according to Exodus 12:40. In the Greek Old Testament
this verse indicated that this period included the time of the patriarchs
in Caanan. Genesis 15:13 and Acts 7:6 give the time in Egypt itself
as 400 years, which may be round numbers instead of exact numbers.

Paul's point was simply that it was a long time, and the covenant of promise had lasted that long without the addition of the law. The giving of the law then did not annul God's promise, especially since it was later fulfilled by Christ. If the giving of the law was intended to provide a new way of receiving God's blessings, then the way of promise would have been eliminated. But God gave his blessings to Abraham, and to Christ his offspring, by promise. Therefore the law was never intended to replace faith in God's promise as the way of salvation. There has never been but one way to be saved, and it is not by keeping the law.

Why the Law? (3:19-20)

Paul had said some very negative things about the law. Now he anticipated that someone would ask, "Why was the law given if it was so ineffective?" Paul suggested two reasons in verse 19. First, "the law was added because of transgressions." Romans 5:13 is the best commentary on this verse. There Paul said that the law made it possible for sin to be counted—that is, there can be no understanding of sin without a standard to measure by. The law was that standard. By providing a track for human behavior, it showed when people were off the track. The law also helped to prepare for the coming of Christ. It was a temporary arrangement of God for man until Christ should come, the offspring of Abraham, who would fulfill the promise of blessing.

Not only was the law a temporary addition; it was not a personal and direct revelation from God in the same way as was the promise to Abraham. The people of Israel did not receive the law directly from God. Moses was an intermediary or go-between. And the Jews of Paul's day also believed that God had dealt with Moses by means of angels (the Greek version of Deut. 33:2 is the only Old Testament source for this idea). When Abraham received the promise only God was involved. This seems to be the meaning of "God is one," although the verse has many varying interpretations. This makes the promise to Abraham a stronger, more basic covenant than the law.

Is the Law Bad? (3:21-22)

At this point the reader may think that the law opposed or contradicted the promise of God. Paul raised this question and answered, "Certainly not," the same strong expression he used in 2:17. The law would be a bad thing if it were given to bring spiritual life and then failed to do so. But no law can bring life. The law was not given for that purpose, so it cannot be judged a failure on that basis. The law, like everything else in human experience, was limited by sin. Paul cited "the scripture" to this effect, but there is no particular verse in the Old Testament that matches his words. Probably he referred to the general teaching of Scripture or to a group of statements such as he quoted in Romans 3:9-18. Because all have sinned, the law cannot bring life. Recognizing this leads persons to see that only faith in Christ can enable them to receive God's promise.

Before and After Christ (3:23-29)

Paul returned to the subject of the purpose of the law. He spoke of the time before faith came. The text actually says "the faith," meaning faith in Christ. Faith had been present all along, as Paul had shown. But before faith in Christ came, Paul and his fellow Jews had been "confined under the law, kept under restraint." "Confined" is literally "being held in custody." "Kept under restraint" is the same word translated "consigned" in verse 22. The idea is that the law was a kind of prison to keep persons under control until the better way of faith was available. In verse 24 Paul used the figure of a custodian. This translates a Greek word which has come over into English as "pedagogue." It refers to a slave who had the duty of exercising moral discipline over a child in ancient Greece. Pictures of these servants show them holding a rod to enforce discipline. The King James Version uses the term "schoolmaster," but the idea of discipline and moral control are probably uppermost here. The King James Version also has "*to bring us* unto Christ," which is not a literal translation as indicated by the use of italics. The Revised Standard Version is more accurate with "until Christ came."

When Christ came, the custodian was no longer necessary. The reason was given in verse 26. Before, the person in question was a minor, a ward under someone else's control. In Christ he is now a son of God by faith. He has entered into full family privileges and partakes of his father's nature. Therefore he does not need the enforced discipline of the guardian. The implication is that a Christian trying to return to the law would be like a mature son wanting to be under the control of a strict governess again.

Verse 27 further described the change that had taken place. Becoming a Christian, described as being "baptized into Christ," meant that a person had put on Christ. He was in a new relationship. Something had happened that made it unnecessary for him to live by the old way of life anymore. The reference to baptism here is a reminder that a new symbol of initiation had taken the place of circumcision. It pointed to death, burial, and new life, not to legal requirements. In this new state of existence the old distinctions no longer applied.

Racial and religious differences were very important in the ancient world, as they are to some today. Jews looked down on Gentiles. Greeks considered non-Greeks as barbarians. The Judaizers wanted to continue to draw the line between Jews and others. But in Christ there is no longer room for such distinctions, Paul said. The Roman Empire was based on the social and economic patterns of slavery. There was all the difference in the world between a slave and a free man—but not in Christ. The early churches included both slaves and free persons in the membership (Eph. 6:5-9; Col. 3:21 to 4:1; Philem. 16).

In the ancient world women were regarded as inferior, as they still are in some areas of our world today. Even Paul set limits at times on the role women were to play in the church. But Paul knew that these were simply temporary limits based on local circumstances. In Christ there is no distinction. All are one. To belong to Christ is to be all that God means for a person to be, a descendant of Abraham, the heir to God's great promise of blessing.

Not Slaves But Sons (4:1-7)

Paul continued to contrast law keeping and living by faith, presenting another illustration drawn from common experience. He described a child who had been left his father's estate but was too young to take possession of it. He was under guardians and trustees. These may have been the overseers set up by Roman law, a guardian or tutor until age fourteen, and a trustee or curator until age twenty-five. Or the terms may have described a personal guardian and a trustee of property who acted at the same time. These officers acted until the time set by the father. Under Roman law the father did not set the time for the son to cease being a minor. It is not certain just which legal system Paul was thinking about, but there were some parallels in Syrian history.

The point here was that the son, until he came of age, was no better off than a slave. He was under the direction of others. We, Paul said, were like that, apparently referring to himself and his readers. Before the coming of Christ, they were slaves to "the elemental spirits of the universe." The King James Version has "elements of the world." This is difficult to interpret, but two basic interpretations are favored. The elements may be elementary principles, religious and moral ABCs such as the Jewish law. Or, as in the Revised Standard Version, they may be the spirits which were thought by the pagans, and perhaps some Jews, to move the heavenly bodies. At any rate, Paul was speaking of people who lived under the yoke of some force other than the Spirit of God as experienced in Christ.

Paul and his fellow believers passed out of their immature bondage when Christ came. As in the illustration where the date was set by the father, Christ came "when the time had fully come"—that is, when God determined that he should come. From the human point of view Jesus was born at a very favorable time. Roman law, Greek language, and Jewish religious teaching all combined to create a situation in which the gospel could spread. But the emphasis is on God's sovereign choice. God sent his Son into the world. This was a gift of grace. He was born of a woman. He shared our human nature. He was born under the law—that is, he was a Jew, and he submitted to the curse that the law imposed. He did this to redeem those who were under the law. The word "redeem" is the same as found in 3:13. He bought or ransomed them out of their bondage.

He also made it possible for them to be adopted as sons of God. Paul might be thinking here of the Roman practice of a man who had no child and who made a slave his heir. This person would cease to be a slave and become a son. But it is more likely that Paul was interested in the experience Christians have of discovering that God is their Father as the Holy Spirit creates the feeling of sonship in their hearts. They find themselves calling God "Father." The term "Abba," used as a synonym for Father, is the Aramaic word a child would have used much as children today use "Daddy." Jesus introduced its use in reference to God. Before that it would have been considered much too familiar and personal. Those who are in Christ enter into this intimate relation with God and inherit the promises of God.

How Can You Turn Back? (4:8-11)

Before the Galatians became Christians, they worshiped the pagan deities. Paul acknowledged their existence as some kind of spirits, but he denied that they were gods. Those who worshiped them were in bondage to them. Then, Paul said, the Galatians came to know God, or, as he would rather put it, to be known by God. This emphasizes the fact that God takes the initiative. Our relationship with him is not, first of all, something we do.

To turn to the works of the law would be to give up this relationship and to return to a state of bondage. Paul implied that bondage to the law would be bondage in the same way that bondage to pagan gods was. Both systems demanded that their followers observe special days and seasons. This would have been one of the appeals that Jewish legalism made to former pagans. Both the works of the law and the pagan gods were "weak and beggarly elemental spirits." Both lacked power to save, and both left persons in dependence and fear. The thought of the Galatians accepting such a condition made Paul feel that he had failed.

An Urgent Plea (4:12-20)

The mention of his work among them in the previous verse led Paul to speak very personally of his ministry in Galatia. He began with a strong appeal, "Become as I am"—that is, free from the law. This he urged because "I also have become as you are." This may mean that Paul had virtually become a Gentile. Or perhaps it referred to the fact that he had once been in bondage to the law as they were in danger of being and had been set free as they were free. In either case, he was saying, "We have a lot in common. I know what you are going through, so follow my example."

What did Paul mean by, "You did me no wrong?" The verb form suggests that they did not wrong him at first, but they had begun to do so. Paul went on to recall how well they had treated him when he first came. He had come to them because of "a bodily ailment." We can only speculate about the nature of his ailment. Since he spoke of their willingness to give him their eyes, he may have suffered from an eye disease. This might also explain the fact that Paul wrote with large letters (Gal. 6:11). Some think that Paul had contracted malaria

in the coastal region of Pamphylia and had come to the higher eleva-
tions of Galatia to get relief. This would explain why the location
was significant. A third view is that Paul suffered from epilepsy. Whatever the illness, it caused Paul to go to Galatia and preach the gospel
there, further evidence that God can bring good out of evil circumstances (see Rom. 8:28).

Paul's condition was a hardship for the Galatians. His care may
have been a burden, or his appearance may have been unpleasant.
But they did not reject him. On the contrary, they accepted him as
they would have an angel or Christ himself. Some think this may
be a reference to the fact that the people of Lystra thought Paul
was Mercury, the messenger of the gods (Acts 14:11-12). Even if that
were in the background, this verse seems to point to hospitality and
respect more than to a superficial impression. The Galatians had felt
very good about having Paul with them. So devoted were they to
Paul that they would have given him their eyes if they could. If
this is not a reference to Paul's eye disease, it may be a general
figure of speech to indicate an intense desire to do something for
Paul.

Comparing this most positive relationship in the beginning with
the betrayal and rejection he now felt, Paul asked, "Have I then become your enemy?" If so, it was only by telling them the truth. If
his preaching of the gospel was so well received in the beginning,
how could he have become their enemy by speaking the same truth
to them?

Paul was apparently speaking of what the Judaizers were saying
about him, for in verse 17 he referred to them. They were eagerly
trying to win the Galatians by giving them a lot of attention. This
would be all right, Paul said, if it were for a good purpose. But the
Judaizers wanted to shut the Galatians out, likely meaning to cut
them off from their ties with Paul. The good purpose may mean the
purpose Paul had when he first came to them.

Verses 19 and 20 are intensely personal. This letter has little affec-
tion or appreciation in it, but here Paul called his readers "My little
children," an unusual term for him, but quite common in the letters
of John. He felt like a parent about to have a child, anxious about
how the child would be and how he would develop. He yearned
for the Galatians to have Christ formed in them, to become truly

Christlike. This, after all, was the test of any approach to religion that claimed to be Christian. He also wished he could be with them so that he could communicate in a more personal way.

A New Look at an Old Story (4:21-31)

Paul now brought his doctrinal argument to a climax. He called for the attention of those who were considering putting themselves under the law and asked whether they had really heard what the law said. After all, Paul was a lifelong student of the law, trained in the schools of the rabbis. He proceeded to point them to the story of Abraham, Sarah, and Hagar (Gen. 16:1 to 18:15; 21:1-21). Abraham and Sarah had no children. Following an accepted practice of the time, they arranged for Abraham to father a child, Ishmael, by Hagar, a servant in their household.

Later God promised that Sarah would bear a child, even though she was now too old. She gave birth to Isaac. Ishmael was born according to the flesh—that is, as the result of Abraham's human efforts. Isaac, however, was born because of God's promise and its fulfillment, in spite of the natural circumstances. Paul told this story in a few brief sentences, without giving the names of the women or the sons. He was more concerned with establishing the two different categories of slave and free. He was talking about two different kinds of people and two different ways of relating to God.

With his emphasis on these categories, Paul told his readers that this was an allegory. "Allegory" is a Greek word carried over into English. It means speaking so as to imply something other than what is literally said. The elements in the story stand for some truth besides the literal meaning. In the strict sense an allegory is interpreted in terms of some hidden meaning that is not even present in the original story. Paul did not seem to use the term in this strict sense because some of the meaning he derived from the story of Abraham was present in the original story. Paul did not deny that there was a real Abraham or that the events were really historical facts. He was saying that they had a spiritual meaning which reached far beyond the original story. This meaning could be seen in their own experience, and Paul proceeded to develop this.

The Jewish rabbis frequently interpreted the Scriptures in this way. They taught that each passage of Scripture had four meanings: the literal, the suggested, the deductive, and the allegorical. Thus Paul was here beating the Judaizers at their own game. He was using the most Jewish manner of teaching to show that the law was not the way to receive the promise. His method may seem strange to modern readers, but his lesson is true.

Since Paul did not ordinarily use this kind of interpretation, it is likely that he was using it here to make a point in the minds of the Galatians and not to say that this was the way all Scripture should be interpreted. Many ancient interpreters tried to read all Scripture in this way, leading to distorted and fanciful understandings. The literal or obvious meaning of a text should always direct our interpretation of the Bible.

The two women stood for two covenants, law and promise. The law covenant, represented by Hagar, came from Mount Sinai. This was where Moses received the law. It was not located in the Promised Land but in Arabia, the area settled by the descendants of Ishmael. Paul linked Hagar with Jerusalem, the center of Judaism and the law. She and her children were slaves. It must have come as a shock to the Judaizers to read this, for the Jews would have said they descended from Isaac, not Ishmael. They thought they were free, not slaves, as they said to Jesus on one occasion (John 8:33). However, Paul was speaking not of biological relationships but spiritual. The Judaizers insisted on the slavery of the law, and the Isaac family was characterized by freedom and promise.

Sarah represented the Jerusalem above, a New Testament designation of the church and the heavenly home of God's people (Heb. 12:22; Rev. 3:12; 21:2,9 ff.) This Jerusalem is free and is the mother of all who are in Christ. Paul broke into a joyful quotation from Isaiah 54:1, in which the fruitfulness of Jerusalem restored was contrasted with the barrenness of Jerusalem destroyed by the conquerors. Sarah had been barren, and the church might seem barren at times; but according to God's promise the children of freedom would be many. Paul reminded the Galatians that they, along with him, belonged in the Isaac family, the family of promise.

Verse 29 adds a further insight. Genesis 21:8-14 speaks of Sarah's displeasure at the continued presence of Ishmael alongside Isaac. Later Jewish tradition spoke of the persecution of Isaac by Ishmael. Paul saw a reenactment of this in the trouble being given the Galatians by the Judaizers. Sarah had demanded that Hagar and Ishmael be sent away. The inheritance could not go to both the slave's son and the free woman's son. Thus Paul was calling for a strong solution to the problem in Galatia. The legalists would have to be cast out. He again reminded the Galatians in verse 31 that they were the children of freedom.

Practical Appeal

5:1 to 6:18

A Passionate Call to Freedom (5:1-12)

These verses began Paul's practical, concluding section. They also summed up what he had said in the previous, doctrinal section. Verse 1 is a transitional sentence, which could easily go with chapter 4, a stirring challenge to embrace freedom, not slavery. "For freedom Christ has set us free" was not just repetition. It pointed to freedom in contrast to all other ways of life. Christ did not die on the cross so that the Galatians could become slaves to the law. "Stand fast" suggests an image of the Galatians about to slip and lose their footing. They were in danger; they must dig in their heels. To accept circumcision would be like an ox permitting the yoke to be placed on his shoulders. "Don't do it!" Paul warned.

Verses 2-3 state two terrible consequences of a lapse into legalism: It would cancel the benefits of Christ for them, and it would put them under the necessity of keeping all of the law. Perhaps the Galatians had not thought of it, but they could not submit to circumcision and stop there. Once they admitted that this was necessary, they would be admitting that all the rest of the law was necessary. As James noted, to break one point of the law was to be guilty of all the law (Jas. 2:10).

Paul amplified further on the other danger. It must have pained him deeply to say it, but he felt that turning to the law would cancel the benefits of Christ in a person's life. The last phrase in verse 2 literally says, "Christ will profit you not one thing." This is so because the way of Christ is a totally different approach to righteousness. If Christ and the law were simply two items in a category of ways to please God, then by all means they should have used both. But the way of the law was the way of human effort, and the way of Christ was the denial of human effort. The two are mutually exclusive.

Verse 4 carries the idea further. To embrace justification by law was to be severed from Christ. Such a person would have removed himself from the relationship in which Christ could benefit him. He would have "fallen away from grace." Because this last phrase has come to mean to some people that a person may be saved through faith in Christ and later lose his salvation through some sin that he commits, it requires careful study. The first thing to note is that Paul was speaking of the catastrophic loss of the benefits of Christ. This clear statement should not be explained away. (It has been suggested, for example, that they would have fallen from sanctifying grace, but not from justifying grace.)

But it is equally clear that Paul was not speaking of losing salvation by committing sin. He was speaking of substituting law for grace as the basis of salvation.

Finally, it should be remembered that Paul was talking about a hypothetical situation. For emphasis he spoke as if they had already fallen from grace. In other places, verses 1-2 for instance, he indicated that they had not yet given in to the legalists. He was simply carrying his argument to its logical conclusion to show them how great the danger was. If they were to give up grace and turn to law, they would not have grace any longer. Paul did not here discuss whether a person who had experienced grace could ever really do such a thing. His concern here was practical guidance, not theoretical argument.

In verse 5 Paul countered their hope for justification through the law with his own hope, which was "through the Spirit, by faith." The promise of righteousness through law is appealing because it is definite and tangible. A person can know that he has it, whatever it is that he has. The righteousness that comes through faith, Paul said, is no less real. It may not be fully experienced until God's final judgment, but it is already present in the form of hope as the Spirit works in the believer now.

Verse 6 is another great key verse. Paul cut through all the debate about circumcision to show what really mattered. Circumcision did not accomplish anything, but neither did uncircumcision. There was no virtue in being circumcised, but neither was there any virtue in

being uncircumcised. It would be an **equally serious error** if the Galatians refused circumcision and then **prided themselves** on that, thinking they had earned some merit in the sight of God. There can be
a legalism of not doing just as there can be a legalism of doing. The
only thing that really counts is "faith working through love."

In response to those who said his way of faith did not require anything definite, Paul pointed out that faith works. But it works through
love, not law. Paul agreed with James here. Some have seen a contra-
diction between Paul's "not of works" (Eph. 2:9) and James' "Faith
. . . if it has no works, is dead" (Jas. 2:17). But Paul clearly stated
here that faith is followed by works (as he did also in Eph. 2:10).

The difference between Paul—or James for that matter—and the
Judaizers was a difference of sequence and source. It is not that works
lead to righteousness. And the righteousness which is by faith can
do works which legalism could never do. The source of real righteousness is in the heart, where only love, not law, can reach. Many a
citizen has sped through school zones in spite of the law. But let
that same citizen have a child in that school, and he will find himself
slowing down. In that case love has brought about an action which
the law could not accomplish.

In this climactic passage, Paul was like a boxer moving in for the
finishing blow. He pulled no punches. He threw everything he had
into it. He tried by every possible means to accomplish his objective.
In verse 7 he reminded his readers how well they had run when
the race first began. Illustrations from athletics were a favorite device
for Paul. He and his readers shared the love of sports that was prominent in Greek and Roman life.

His next tactic was to force the Galatians to think about the person
or persons who had brought about the change in their thinking. They
had not taken this direction on their own. Someone had hindered,
literally "cut in." This had tragically kept them from obeying the
truth. Such a change in thinking could not have come from God,
the one who called them. The evil influence had spread in their lives
like leaven working its way through a lump of dough. This was apparently a proverb current in Paul's day. He used it in 1 Corinthians
5:6 to refer to the effect of immorality. Leaven or yeast was a symbol
of evil influence throughout the New Testament (with the exception
of Matt. 13:33 and Luke 13:21).

In spite of the defection in Galatia, Paul's faith in God gave him

hope that the Galatians would agree with him. This expression of
confidence would, of course, put pressure on the Galatians to live
up to it. Paul anticipated that the evil workers (the singular in v. 10
is a general reference to any and all who trouble them) would be
judged wrong, both by the Galatians and by God.

One further issue remained to be dealt with. Strange as it may
seem, the Judaizers had actually contended that Paul did teach the
requirement of circumcision. Perhaps Timothy had already been circumcised (Acts 16:1-3) and they had heard of it. But Timothy was
the son of a Jewish woman, and Paul's circumcision of him was to
affirm Timothy's Jewish heritage, not to teach justification through
the law. Paul countered such an accusation by pointing to the persecution he suffered from the Jews. No, he still preached salvation based
on the cross, or he would not encounter such opposition. It was the
Judaizers, as seen in 6:12, who sought to escape persecution by enforc-
ing circumcision and playing down the cross.

Verse 12 is the strongest statement in the epistle, and it showed
how deeply disturbed Paul was over this crisis. He expressed the wish
that the troublemakers in Galatia would "mutilate themselves." The
language here leaves no doubt that Paul was referring to castration
or emasculation. This was actually practiced in the frenzied worship
of the goddess Cybele in the area of Galatia. Paul was pointing to
the eunuch priests of Cybele who were well known to his readers
and saying, "If circumcision seems so important to the Judaizers, is
there really any difference between them and these poor pagans?"

Freedom Through Loving Service (5:13-15)

Paul repeated his challenge once again. As in verse 1, he pointed
to freedom. As in verse 8 he reminded them of their calling. As he
had done several times before (3:15; 4:12,31) he called them brethren.
Then, having made his point about freedom, he turned to clarify
what that freedom means. There is always the danger that freedom
will be mistaken for license. It could become, Paul said, "an occasion"
(KJV, a military term meaning a base of operations) "for the flesh."
By flesh Paul meant human nature without the motivation of the
Holy Spirit. He would shortly spell out just what the works of the
flesh were.

If the Christian is not under the law, then what is to prevent him
from giving in to the desires of the flesh? Why, the commitment to

be servants of one another through love! This is what the law is all about. If you love your neighbor as yourself (Lev. 19:18; Luke 10:27), then you have kept the law (Rom. 13:8-10). Thus Paul showed that he did not deny what the law aimed at, which was righteousness. He simply said that the law cannot bring it about; but Christ can.

Life without such a commitment to love would be chaos and destruction. This is true of legalism as well as license. Without love persons would "bite and devour one another" like wild animals tearing at each other's throats. Thus, like the gingham dog and the calico cat, they would eat each other up.

Walk by the Spirit (5:16-24)

Paul had just described the kind of life that lapses into uncontrolled indulgence of the flesh. He now presented the Christian alternative, which is not law but Spirit. Paul used a present-tense verb which means "keep on walking by the Spirit." The description of the Christian life as walking was common in the New Testament. It emphasized the practical, daily results of being in Christ. By "Spirit" he meant the presence and power of God in the believer's life.

The contrary alternative which Paul rejected would be to gratify the desires of the flesh. In the Greek text of verse 17 the word translated "desires are" is a verb. Thus the King James Version, "lusteth," is more accurate. What the flesh wants opposes the Spirit, and what the Spirit wants opposes the flesh. The believer caught in this conflict finds that he cannot do what he wants to do. The solution is to give in to the Spirit's leadership, not to submit to the law. Those who are led by the Spirit are not under the law. They have something better than the law to control their behavior.

In case his readers might not know what he meant by the flesh, Paul offered a list of fifteen works of the flesh. The term in general means human nature apart from the control of the Spirit; thus it described humanity's lower nature. A close look at the list will show that works of the flesh are not just physical. Flesh includes all elements of life—attitudes and relationships as well as physical deeds, mind and soul as well as body.

The first three works of the flesh are closely related. "Fornication" refers to improper sexual relations. The Greek root here is *porn*, from which the English word pornography comes. "Impurity," meaning uncleanness, was a more general term for immorality. "Licentiousness" described looseness or wantonness, especially in sexual relations. In the pagan world of the first century, the uncontrolled expression of sex was not only condoned; it was a part of the worship of the gods. Paul found it necesssary to speak out strongly against this for religious as well as moral reasons. Such things did not come from the Spirit, as the pagans believed, but from man's lower nature, the flesh. Modern society bears a striking resemblance to the ancient world in this respect. The so-called new morality is often simply a new paganism—the old immorality in a new guise.

The next two items are interrelated and involve religious practices. "Idolatry" was the acceptance of substitutes for the true God. "Sorcery" was the practice of magic. The word for sorcery here is the Greek word from which we get "pharmacy" and means the use of medicine and drugs. In the ancient world, medicine and magic were mixed together. In pagan worship, the sorcerer used his potions to counterfeit the work of the Holy Spirit. Paul encountered one such person, Elymas, on his first missionary journey (Acts 13:4-12).

The next eight items on the list have to do with problems of social relationships. Of the eight, the first, second, sixth, and seventh describe division and conflict. "Enmity" is a general word for hostility. "Strife" describes more outward and active fighting. "Dissension" is literally "standing apart" and describes the formation of splinter groups. "Party spirit" translates the Greek word from which we get "heresy." The term in Greek was not originally bad. It meant choosing. But when people hold different views, they often come to dislike each other; and in this sense the formation of conflicting opinions is a work of the flesh. The answer is not that persons should always agree, but that they should disagree without being disagreeable.

The other four problems of social relationships are mental attitudes which destroy community. "Jealousy" can mean zeal. Here it means zeal of the wrong kind. It is eagerness to have what someone else has. "Anger," in the sense used here, means bursts of temper rather than a set attitude of anger. "Selfishness" is more accurately ambition or self-seeking. Thus it is an active, destructive kind of selfishness. "Envy" refers to an embittered spirit that does not want others to enjoy good things.

The last two vices had to do with both social life and religious life. "Drunkenness" was actually condoned in the worship of Bacchus and was a danger that was frequently described in the Bible. "Carousing" describes the unrestrained revelry that takes place when pleasure seeking goes out of control. In Ephesians 5:18 Paul specifically contrasted drunkenness with being filled with the Spirit. Having listed fifteen vices, Paul added "and the like" to show that these are just a sample of the many he could have mentioned.

He also added a warning that he had given to the Galatians before, probably during his first ministry with them. Pagan converts would need much instruction and emphasis in the area of ethics. They needed to know how foreign such behavior was to the kingdom of God. Therefore Paul told them that "those who do such things shall not inherit the kingdom of God." The kingdom of God is the rule of God at the end of time and also its presence already in the lives of believers. Participation in this kingdom means control by the Spirit. It excluded a life which is controlled by the flesh and which manifested this control in works such as Paul had described.

The qualities produced by the Spirit in the life of God's people provide a pleasant contrast to the sorry catalog of the works of the flesh. Instead of "works," the Spirit's qualities are "fruit." They grow out of the work of the Spirit. Only nine are listed. Whereas the works of the flesh are many in number but poor in quality, the fruit of the Spirit are few in number but boundlessly rich in quality.

"Love," "joy," and "peace" head the list. All are inner, spiritual qualities, but they are also shared with others. "Love" is mentioned first. This agreed with Paul's teaching in 1 Corinthians 13 that love is the greatest virtue. It also reminded the reader that love fulfills the intention of the law (5:13-14). "Joy," while not prominent in Galatians, was a major feature of Paul's letter to the Philippians. "Peace" appears in all of Paul's letters, especially in the salutation where it accompanies grace. It is a great general word to describe all that God does in the believer's life (see the discussion of 1:3).

The last six manifestations of the fruit of the Spirit are more concerned with the Christian's dealings with others and his practical conduct of his own life. "Patience" means specifically endurance, the ability to bear up under difficulty. It is used mostly with regard to people and frequently in relation to God's attitude toward human beings. "Kindness" and "goodness" are similar in meaning. "Goodness" may be a more active form of behavior. It can show strength as well as sweetness. "Faith" seems to have the idea of faithfulness or trustworthiness here. "Gentleness" suggests mildness or submission to the will of God. The King James Version translates it as "meekness," but this word has come to be too weak in general usage. It is used in secular Greek to describe an animal that has been tamed and brought under control. Thus it does not mean weakness so much as gentle, controlled strength. "Self-control" is mastery over oneself. It is used of an athlete's discipline (1 Cor. 9:25) and of sexual restraint (1 Cor. 7:9). These virtues, Paul said, are not restricted by law. They are beyond the power of law to produce and beyond the need of law to control. These are the characteristics of those who belong to Christ. The other things, the works of the flesh, have no place in their lives. When they joined Christ they submitted the flesh with all its drives to death in his cross.

In verse 25 he repeated the challenge to walk by the Spirit, offering as reason for this the fact that we live by the Spirit. Through the Spirit believers have life. They exist in a vital relationship with God. But the outworking of this life does not come automatically. There must be constant application, described as walking, in order to develop the implications of spiritual life. Verse 26 offers a practical example. Paul was saying that, since all forms of strife are works of the flesh, and since the Spirit produces such fruits as we have described, then let's put this truth to work. Let's do away with selfishness, provocation, and envy. This, he was saying, is the kind of behavior change I have in mind. To make this change would be walking in the Spirit.

Practical Spirituality (6:1-10)

To make his illustration even more specific, Paul used a case study. He may have heard that some Galatian Christian had done wrong and had been harshly judged. He said that in such a case the spiritual thing to do was to restore the person in a gentle way. "Restore" was a term used of fishermen mending their nets or of a physician setting a broken bone. Those who conduct this kind of ministry will not do so with pride. They will be aware that they too are liable to sin. Therefore, they will keep constant watch on themselves lest they fall into temptation. Living by the Spirit is no guarantee that one will not be tempted.

Being spiritual does not mean giving all one's attention to one's own condition. It requires concern and responsibility for others. Christians are to bear one another's burdens (a word meaning heavy weights). In the family of faith, difficulties are to be shared. They are not private property.

In contrast to the spiritual person who bears the burdens of others, the flesh-controlled person is wrapped up in himself. The lure of legalism is that it enables a person to pride himself on the fact that he is doing more than others. This creates a false estimate of self, based on competitive comparing. Paul said such a person may actually think he has a certain virtue when he does not have it at all. He is fooling himself.

The answer is for each person to test his own work, not just to compare himself to others or to some standard they have agreed on. Let him give an objective evaluation of his behavior and see if it has any validity in and of itself. Then if he finds something good, he can be glad about that and not about some supposed superiority over his neighbor. Even though Christians are to bear each other's burdens (heavy weights, v. 2), there is a certain responsibility each must bear for himself. Paul called this individual responsibility a "load," a word which was used to refer to a soldier's pack.

Another practical matter of behavior was introduced by Paul as an example of spiritual responsibility. Christians who are taught by a teacher are to contribute to his support. Paul may have feared that the mention of each person carrying his own load in verse 5 would lead the Galatians to abandon the support of those who ministered to him. There seems to have been developing in the early church a group of teachers who gave enough time to this important task that they required some support from the congregation. Paul himself believed that he had a right to support from those whom he served. He accepted help from the Philippians because they wanted to share in his ministry, but he refused support from the Corinthians because he was being accused of taking advantage of them (Phil. 4:14-18; 1 Cor. 9:6-18; 2 Cor. 11:7-11).

In verses 7-10 Paul countered a possible objection. The kind of spiritual living he had been describing did not always produce quick, visible results. Obeying the law was a thing that could be measured and enjoyed. Indulging the flesh brought quick pleasure. But what if one practiced patience and meekness and had nothing to show for it? Paul answered by pointing to a basic spiritual principle. God must be taken into account and his word respected. A further principle was that persons reap what they sow. If someone's life was invested in the concerns of the flesh, he would reap corruption. But if his life was invested in the things of the Spirit, there would be a harvest of eternal life.

So to those who became discouraged at the lack of quick, visible results in the spiritual life, Paul said, "Let us not grow weary in well-doing, for in due season we shall reap, if we do not lose heart." It will not be easy. It may take a long time. But the Spirit produces his fruit. Once again, in verse 10, Paul reminded them that he was talking about such practical things as doing good to others, all others, and especially fellow church members.

Conclusion (6:11-18)

Paul called attention to the large letters with which he was writing. Most interpreters suppose that he was using a secretary or amanuensis to write his letter and at the end wrote his own conclusion to personalize it. However, it is possible that he wrote the entire letter and near the end spoke of the large handwriting. The largeness of the letters may refer to bold strokes he was using for emphasis, or to the contrast between his own handwriting and the neater hand of a professional scribe, or to a weakness of Paul's eyesight which caused him to write large.

He repeated now in his own handwriting the essential point of his message. Those who wanted to force circumcision on the Galatians did not have high motives. They wanted to look good in the eyes of other Jews and to avoid persecution by evading the straightforward message of the cross. They did not even keep the law themselves. No one was able to. They just wanted the glory of having brought about a certain number of circumcisions.

Paul would have none of this. With the same phrase of strong denial he had used before (2:17; 3:21) he rejected the idea of boasting in anything except the cross of Christ. It was by this cross that he died to the world and its superficial standards. And by the cross the world became dead as far as he was concerned. In view of the absolute priority of the cross, circumcision and uncircumcision were unimportant. He had said this in 5:6. There the thing that counted, he said, was faith working through love. Here he said that it was a new creation. The two are aspects of the same thing, the saving activity of God in his life. He pronounced a blessing of peace and mercy to all

who followed this rule—that is, the centrality of God's saving act in
the cross. These, he said, and not those who practice circumcision,
were the Israel of God. This was likely a reference to Psalm 125:5,
"Peace be in Israel!" But here, for Paul, the church was the new
Israel.

Having said all that needed to be said, Paul stopped with simple
words. The issue was settled as far as he was concerned. He said in
effect, "Don't bother me anymore." His ground for saying this was
that he had the marks of Christ on his body, the scars of beatings
and stonings which the Galatians had seen. As always, he pronounced
a blessing at the end. To the Galatians it is especially appropriate:
"The grace of our Lord Jesus Christ be with your spirit, brethren."
He reminded them of grace. He reminded them that they were spiritual beings. He reminded them that they were his brothers. Paul did
not always put "Amen" at the end of his letters (only in Romans
besides Galatians). At the end of this urgent, demanding epistle he
felt like saying "Amen." So be it!

Notes

1. George S. Duncan, *The Epistle of Paul to the Galatians*, "The Moffatt
New Testament Commentary" (London: Hodder and Stoughton, 1934), p. xvi.
2. A. M. Hunter, *The Letter of Paul to the Galatians*, etc., "The Layman's
Bible Commentary" (Richmond: The John Knox Press, 1959), p. 11.

EPHESIANS

Introduction

Ephesians is special. Granted, "All scripture is inspired by God and profitable" (2 Tim. 3:16), but even within Scripture there are high points. A traveler may have seen many beautiful mountain views, but when he comes to the Alps he says, "Here is a place to stop for a while and gaze." Similarly, many students of the Bible have given special attention to Ephesians. Here the teachings of Paul find their highest expression in a sweeping summary of his faith. The mood of the book is one of great confidence and assurance. Its positive affirmations are given with no note of conflict to distract. Its insight is profound and powerful. It gives the impression of being the most modern book in the Bible because it is written in terms that are both timeless and timely. Its language is majestic and poetic. Because Ephesians is different from other biblical writings, we have to stop and deal with some special questions that have been raised about this book.

Author

Twice the author gave his name: "Paul, an apostle of Jesus Christ" (1:1) and "I, Paul, a prisoner for Christ Jesus" (3:1). He described himself by saying, "I am an ambassador in chains" (6:20). Even if Paul's name were not given, many of the ideas and words in Ephesians would be recognized as his. There is a particularly strong resemblance between Ephesians and Colossians. Furthermore, Christian writers from earliest times accepted Ephesians as the work of Paul. This was not questioned until late in the eighteenth century.

In modern times many scholars have wondered whether Ephesians was really written by Paul. They point to the fact that a large number of the words used in Ephesians do not occur in the other letters of Paul. Moreover, even the ideas common to Paul are developed and applied in ways not found in the other Pauline epistles. And, unlike the other letters, Ephesians has none of the local references and particular problems that usually concerned the great missionary writer.

Such considerations have led many to conclude that someone else wrote Ephesians. This person, they say, knew Paul's writings well and wrote to summarize them.

Perhaps, it is suggested, Ephesians was written by the man who gathered the other letters of Paul and began to circulate them as a group. It would then serve as a summary and an introduction to the collected writing of Paul. The use of Paul's name would be justified on the grounds that the ideas were Paul's ideas and the writing was accompanied by the other writings of Paul. It is even possible that someone did this under the direction of Paul himself. We do know that Paul used secretaries at times to write his correspondence (Rom. 16:22), a practice common in the ancient world as well as today.

On the other hand, many capable scholars continue to hold the traditional view that the author is Paul himself. They point out that it is unlikely there was "a second Paul," someone capable of equaling and even surpassing the gifted apostle while remaining unknown himself. All that the letter said about its author (the internal evidence) and all that the church has said about it for almost two thousand years (the external evidence) points to Paul. The differences in vocabulary and thought could be explained in other ways. If there was another author, it might help our understanding of early church history to know about him; but it would not change our understanding of the message of Ephesians. This commentary will proceed on the assumption, backed by strong evidence, that Ephesians is the work of Paul himself.

Destination

The King James Version of Ephesians 1:1 includes the words "to the saints which are at Ephesus," but the oldest manuscripts of this writing do not include a place name. The Revised Standard Version follows the strong manuscript evidence as well as statements from early Christian writers in saying simply, "to the saints who are also faithful in Christ Jesus." So the letter itself does not tell us who the intended readers were.

Paul knew the Christians at Ephesus well. He had spent three years preaching the gospel there (Acts 19; 20:31). He had strong feelings and deep friendship toward the leaders of the church there (Acts 20:36-38). It would be strange if he had written a major epistle to them without any personal references. Yet Ephesians tells us nothing about the relationship of Paul and the readers. Several statements in the letter imply that Paul did not know the readers well (1:15; 3:2; 4:20-21).

The most likely explanation of all this is that the letter we know as Ephesians was written to a more general audience. The similarity to Colossians suggests that it was written soon after that letter and was sent to the same area. We know that Paul's work at Ephesus influenced the entire Roman province of Asia (Acts 19:10), which today is the western part of Turkey. In addition to the churches at Ephesus and Colossae, there were the others listed in the book of Revelation (Smyrna, Pergamum, Thyatira, Sardis, Philadelphia, and Laodicea).

Perhaps, having written to the Colossians such a strong statement of the fullness of Christ (Col. 1:15-20) and the revelation of the mystery concerning the salvation of the Gentiles (Col. 1:27 to 2:3), Paul decided to share these themes with the other churches by means of a circular letter carried around by Tychicus (Eph. 6:22), who also delivered the letter to Colossae (Col. 4:7). It has even been suggested that each copy had a blank for Tychicus to insert the name of the church when he delivered it and that the copy at Ephesus came to be the best known because this was the leading church. This theory has the disadvantage that no place names are found in the best ancient manuscripts. It is more likely that the letter was simply addressed to "saints" in general, although other circular letters name the various churches (Rev.) or the area (2 Cor.; Gal.; 1 Pet.).

Date

Those who doubt that Paul wrote Ephesians think that the letter was written at the time that Paul's writings were collected and widely circulated around A.D. 90. There is evidence that Ephesians was known by other writers by 96. Those who hold the traditional view of Pauline authorship date the letter during Paul's imprisonment at Rome, 60-62. He referred to himself as "an ambassador in chains" (6:20).

Contents

Ephesians follows the general pattern, common to Paul's letters, of discussing doctrine in the first half and practice in the last half of the book. Chapters 1—3 spell out the great Christian truths of experience and belief. Chapters 4—6 describe how Christians should live in the light of these truths. The discussion does not follow the logical outline of an argument as does Romans or a sequence of subjects as does 1 Corinthians. It is more like a symphony in which themes are stated, left for a while, and picked up later, often to be woven in with other themes.

There are many similarities with Colossians. One-third of the words found in Colossians are also used in Ephesians. Ephesians 6:21-22 is an exact quotation of Colossians 4:7-8. There are also echoes of the other Pauline epistles throughout Ephesians. Ephesians is a summary of Paul's teachings with special emphasis on the church and the Christian life. In common with Colossians, there is more of an emphasis on the cosmic role of Christ, his superiority over the whole universe, including any other spiritual powers that might exist. This is in contrast to the heresies that were present in the Roman Empire of that time, which honored a whole hierarchy of spiritual powers. These teachings, later known as gnosticism (from the Greek word for knowledge), offered salvation to a spiritual elite who shared their special brand of knowledge. Ephesians shows Christ to be the source of the revelation that explains the ultimate mystery of salvation.

But Ephesians is more concerned to show how the revelation of God's purpose in Christ relates to the church and to the lives of the people in the church. Addressed to Gentile Christians, the letter reminds them that they are one with the Jewish believers who first shared the gospel with them. It also reminds them that they have been called to a new quality of life that is sharply different from the immoral ways so common in paganism.

The stately language of Ephesians has led many to think that it was written with public worship in mind. Instead of the argumentative style usually seen in Paul's letters, there is more of declaration and proclamation in Ephesians. It reads well in public worship, and this may have been in Paul's mind as he wrote. The prevailing mood is one of positive assurance.

Ephesians reads more like a sermon than a letter. It is put in letter form because this was the style Paul used in sending his writings to the churches. But in this document Paul was not concerned with personal statements or local conditions. He was not dealing with a particular crisis, so the mood was one of calm but powerful reflection.

The theme of the book is the purpose of God fulfilled in Christ.

This purpose has been accomplished in the lives of believers who have been brought from death to life and sealed with the Spirit. It has also been accomplished in the church which includes believers, both Jew and Gentile, in a unified spiritual organism. This purpose of God takes the form of a high calling which requires the response of changed lives.

Relevance for Today

Ephesians has been called the most modern of all the New Testament writings. The breadth and depth of its theological statement make it a lively source of ideas for every situation. Its emphasis on the all-inclusive nature of the church makes it a rich source of inspiration and challenge for churches of any age. Its stress on Christ's unifying, reconciling work makes it especially attractive to a world that knows the iron curtain, the Berlin Wall, and racial barriers.

Christ for the whole universe.—The New Testament writers could not have envisioned our age of space flights and satellites, but they had no doubt that Christ was big enough to be Lord of the whole creation. He was "far above all rule and authority and power and dominion, and above every name that is named, not only in this age but in that which is to come; and he has put all things under his feet and has made him the head over all things" (Eph. 1:21-22). Ephesians is one of the major sources for our vision of Christ as the Lord of all creation.

The nature and purpose of the church.—No book of the Bible gives a more exalted vision of the church than Ephesians, and none has had a greater impact on modern church life and theory. The vision of the church as the body of Christ in which gifts are recognized and the leaders equip the people for the work of ministry has been rekindled in the twentieth century by the study of the book of Ephesians.

Bringing together a divided world.—Ephesians tells us that God's plan is "to unite all things in him" (1:10). It envisions a world in which God and man have been reconciled. It sets forth a church in which both Jews and Gentiles join in one faith, serving one Lord. Dividedness is still a dominant characteristic of human life. Society still knows divisions of black and white, young and old, male and female, labor and management, liberal and conservative, Republican and Democrat, dictatorships and free societies. The message of peace and unified purpose in Christ is most pertinent to the modern world.

A sense of calling.—Ephesians challenges the best in humanity with "the calling to which you have been called" (4:1). Both institutions and individuals today lack a sense of purpose. Even churches sometimes languish because they lack a compelling goal. The view of life offered by Ephesians is one of strong motivation to get involved in what God is doing in the world.

Worthy living.—"Life-style" has become a common term today. Our culture is "pluralistic." There is said to be a "new morality." Traditional moral values are widely questioned and abandoned. The book of Ephesians describes Christian living as walking in light in a world of darkness. It presents a convincing case for a radically different life-style for Christians. Appropriate patterns of behavior are described in detail.

God's Great Plan
1:1 to 3:21

Salutation (1:1-2)

The opening words of Ephesians are in the standard form for letters of the day (see comments on 2 Cor. 1:1-2 and Gal. 1:1-3). Several matters included in this salutation have already been discussed in the Introduction.

Paul identified himself as "an apostle." This term, originally meaning one who is sent, is equivalent to missionary. In the early church it soon came to identify the twelve disciples of Jesus, including Matthias who replaced Judas. It is used of others, however, and Paul consistently used it of himself. In addition to identifying him as one sent on a mission by Christ, the term also points to his authority to speak as an inspired leader. His apostleship is "by the will of God." It did not come to him through any human agent, as his critics sometimes suggested (see especially Gal.). The mention of the will of God at this point is also significant because it is a major theme of Ephesians. God is a God of purpose, and he calls his servants to take part in accomplishing his purpose.

The Revised Standard Version follows the best early manuscripts in omitting the name "Ephesus" in verse 1. The grammatical form of the sentence is interpreted by some as indicating that there was a place name here or space left for one. Without the name the words are difficult to translate smoothly.

The readers were identified simply as "saints." The word means "holy people." In biblical usage "holy" means set apart for God, so they were God's people. This was a way of saying that they were a continuation of the Old Testament people of God. Israel was to be a holy nation (Ex. 19:5-6; Lev. 19:1-2; Deut. 7:6; 14:2). This calling has been handed on to the church, which is made up of "saints," holy or set-apart ones. Thus the Bible does not use the term in the sense of a select few whose dedication surpasses that of ordinary Christians. "Saints" was a name for all Christians. The saints to whom Ephesians was addressed were also said to be faithful. This could have two meanings, and perhaps both are intended here. They were those who had faith in Christ, and they showed fidelity or loyalty in their service of Christ.

"In Christ" was an expression Paul used frequently. In various forms it occurs thirty-five times in Ephesians. Depending on how it was used in each case, it can be interpreted in at least three ways. Sometimes it simply means "Christian"—that is, belonging to Christ. At other times it means "by means of Christ," since he is the one who brings about the blessings of salvation. It may have the idea of "in the community of Christ"—that is, being a part of the church, the corporate people of God. But quite often it has a deeper spiritual sense of union and fellowship with Christ. Those who exercise faith in Christ are brought into living relation with him. By faith they participate in his death and in his life. This does not mean they lose their own individual identity as in Oriental mysticism. But it does mean that Christ gives a new context and a new motivating power to their lives. Christianity is first of all a personal relationship with Christ the living Lord.

"Grace and peace" comprised the usual greeting in Paul's letters (see the salutations of 2 Cor. and Gal.). The idea of peace would be prominent later in Ephesians (2:13-17) as Paul discussed the reconciling work of Christ. He has made peace between God and man and also between man and man. The ultimate source of this grace and peace is God the Father. The immediate source is the Lord Jesus

Christ. This threefold name for the Son of God is significant. "Jesus" is his given name, meaning "the Lord is salvation" (Matt. 1:21). "Christ" is the Greek equivalent of Messiah or anointed one. It is the title that describes his role in fulfilling the prophecies of the Old Testament. This would not have been fully appreciated by the Gentiles, but the other title, "Lord," was very familiar to them. It was commonly used by the Greeks for masters of slaves and for the emperor.

God Who Has Blessed Us (1:3-14)

The body of Ephesians begins with a great statement of praise to God for his blessings. This way of expressing blessing to God was a familiar form of prayer among the Jews. In the original Greek this passage was one long sentence of twelve verses, but modern translations break it up into several shorter sentences. This is helpful, but it is good to remember that the whole section was intended to flow in a single sweep of praise for all the benefits of salvation.

The Father's purpose (1:3-6).—Christian faith and experience begin with God and always come back to God. Theology was here stated in terms of prayer and praise. God is both the one who blesses and the one who is to be blessed. He is known through his revelation in Christ; hence he is identified as "the God and Father of our Lord Jesus Christ." Jesus spoke of God as his Father, and through him believers come to know God as their Father (v. 5). In this relationship they discover they have "every spiritual blessing." This manifold blessing as described in Ephesians includes election, adoption, redemption, forgiveness, revelation, and the Holy Spirit.

Such blessings are not simply earthly, human experiences. They exist "in the heavenly places." There is no word meaning "places" in the original. The text reads simply "heavenlies," which probably means in the spiritual realm. The Bible witnesses to a dimension of spiritual reality beyond the world we experience with the five senses. Heaven is a future promise for believers, but in Christ they already experience the reality of his power over the world.

Not only do believers now experience the spiritual blessings of Christ, but this was God's plan for them even before he made the world. Paul was deeply convinced that his salvation and Christian life were God's idea and not his. All of this came about because of God's love and grace, not because of Paul's own accomplishment.

He expressed awe and wonder that God has chosen him. It was a mystery that had no explanation except God's sovereign will. He had a deep sense of confidence that the whole process was in God's hands. He did not say that he had no freedom to choose or that there was anyone else who was left out of God's plan. Such conclusions are the result of misinterpreting what Paul said. It is also important to note that the purpose of God's prior choice of the believer is "that we should be holy and blameless." Election (the theological term for this prior choice) is not just to privilege but also to responsibility. No one can rest on his election by grace as an excuse for neglecting responsible action.

The motive behind God's plan is love. The Revised Standard Version places the phrase "in love" in verse 5 with "destined" rather than in verse 4 with "before him." God's loving purpose aims at a personal relationship. Christians are "his sons through Christ," an idea also found in Romans 8:29, where Christ was described as the elder brother and the other brothers are like him.

The result of this plan is praise. The term "to the praise of his glorious grace" contains repetition for the sake of emphasis. When Christians realize what God has done, they want to praise him for it. His glory is shown in his grace and reflected back in praise. This, too, takes place in Christ, who is here called "the Beloved." This term for the Messiah was familiar to the Jews and was the term which the disciples heard as the Father expressed his approval of Jesus his Son (Mark 1:11).

The accomplishment of Christ (1:7-10).—Having moved in his expression of praise to think of Christ, Paul now described what Christ has done for us. He has brought "redemption." This is a term that occurs throughout the Old Testament. There it refers to buying back something which was one's former property, a slave or a piece of land. In the New Testament it retains some of this sense and becomes a key word for salvation in the sense of deliverance or setting free. The form of the word used here is a compound word that contains the same word Jesus used in Mark 10:45 when he said he came "to give his life as a *ransom* for many."

This purchase of deliverance was made at great cost, "through his blood." The blood was a reference to the death of Jesus on the cross with emphasis on the sacrificial meaning of his death. Redemption also has a great result in the lives of Christians, "the forgiveness of our trespasses." The word for "forgiveness" basically means "removal" or setting free. "Trespasses" in this passage was the word for false steps or deviation from the right. The more general word for sin in the New Testament meant missing the mark (both are used in 2:1).

All of this happens not because of any human accomplishment, but "according to the riches of his grace." Redemption is God's free gift to man, and he has the "riches," the spiritual resources, to give such a great gift. Paul spoke of riches six times in Ephesians (see also 1:18; 2:4,7; 3:8,16). God's provision of grace is both generous and impressive. He does not just give it in meager amounts; he lavishes it on his people.

Some translations (KJV, NEB) take the phrase "in all wisdom and insight [or prudence]" along with the verb "lavished" in verse 8. These would then be human characteristics which God gives by his grace. The Revised Standard Version (also TEV) takes the terms with "[has] made known" in verse 9, considering them as God's wisdom and insight in the process of revelation. The two terms are close synonyms, but the Greeks distinguished between them. "Wisdom" is the ability to see into the heart of things and understand them. "Insight" or "prudence" is understanding which leads to wise action.

The passage reached a high point as Paul described what God made known in Christ. This is nothing less than "the mystery of his will." "Mystery" was a word which was common on the religious scene of the first century. Cults known as mystery religions were built around secret spiritual lore known only to a few. A movement called gnosticism was developing in which salvation was offered to a select few who shared in their special knowledge. Paul countered these teachings with a different view of "mystery" in Colossians and Ephesians. This mystery was not something hidden but something made known. It was a mystery in the sense that it was previously unknown. It could only be known by a revelation from God, but in Christ just such a revelation is available.

The content of the mystery was the will and purpose of God. This purpose was "set forth in Christ." Apart from Christ it could not be known. Only as people receive Christ and begin to see life in the light of his revelation do they realize what God is working to do in human lives.

God was pursuing "a plan for the fullness of time." All along he had a strategy in mind which he would accomplish when the time was right. The word for "plan" (KJV, "dispensation") is the Greek word from which we get "economy." It literally means "house rule" and refers to the administration of the house or the responsibility of running a household. Thus it meant God's governing of the world and his arranging of events. This plan was unfolded at a particular time, not haphazardly. This word for "time" means a particular time of opportunity, not just the passing of days and years.

God plans "to unite all things in him." "Unite" translates a word meaning to gather together and present as a whole. The Greeks added a column of figures and put the sum at the top. This word described that process. It was also used to describe a speaker summing up a speech. It portrayed here the unifying of all things with Christ as the head. The ancient Gnostics believed that the physical creation was inferior to the spiritual. They pictured many spiritual powers, some in opposition to Christ and some as mediators between God and the world. Paul said that all of reality, both physical and spiritual, would be included in the unity in Christ.

Future life in the Spirit (1:11-14).—Paul continued to emphasize the working out of God's purpose in Christ. God was described as the "one who accomplishes all things according to the counsel of his will." This means that God is able to do what he wants to do. It also means that the experience of God's people at any given time is not all there is. It is a part of an ongoing plan that includes all things. It included the early Jewish Christians like Paul ("we who first hoped in Christ"). They were chosen to be God's new people and to accomplish God's purpose in their lives. The fact that this was God's doing was emphasized by two words which are not clearly translated in the Revised Standard Version. The main verb means "chosen to be God's portion," as Israel was made God's special people. The participle with this verb means "being predestined." Both show that God had planned for those who believe in Christ to constitute the new people of God.

This new people also includes the Gentiles. In verse 13 the pronoun changes from "we" to "you." Paul was thinking of second-generation converts, and most of these were Gentiles. They had heard the Christian message. This was described as "the word of truth." It contained the knowledge of God's revelation. It was also "the gospel of your salvation." It was good news because it offered forgiveness of sins.

These converts not only heard; they believed, which is always the proper response to the gospel. When they did this, they "were sealed with the promised Holy Spirit." A seal was a mark, perhaps on wax, that showed that something was authentic and had been delivered intact. The evidence that a person has come to be in Christ is the working of the Holy Spirit in his life.

The Holy Spirit is also a down payment or foretaste of final salvation. The word "guarantee" translates a Greek word which was used of security that was put down in a business transaction to assure that the goods would be delivered. Through the Spirit we have already an advance experience of what we shall have fully in heaven. The final possession of the inheritance in verse 14 may apply to the believer who possesses his inheritance or to God who takes final possession. The King James Version has a more literal translation that shows how the Greek leaves both options open: "until the redemption of the purchased possession."

For a third time it was emphasized that all this is "to the praise of his glory." By the unfolding of this plan, God's nature was seen to be glorious; and his people were moved to praise him.

A Prayer for the Readers (1:15-23)

Reasons for the prayer (1:15-16).—Mention of the faith of the Ephesians in verse 13 led Paul to focus on his readers. It was customary to include a prayer for the readers in ancient letters, but this was more than a customary prayer. Paul did not seem to know these readers personally. He had heard of their faith and love, perhaps through Epaphras, as in Colossians 1:4-8. Faith and love belong together in Paul's thought (Gal. 5:6), but some early manuscripts omit "love" in this verse. Faith is our reception of God's grace. Love is our sharing it with others. Whatever the apostle's relationship with these Christians, he prayed for them. His prayers were continuous and intense. They were characterized by thanksgiving.

Prayer for understanding (1:17-19).—The prayer was addressed to God in his relation to Jesus Christ as in 1:3. He was further described as "the Father of glory," probably meaning "the all-glorious Father" (NEB). This is in line with the emphasis of this chapter on the fullness and richness of God's nature and blessings.

The first request was for "a spirit of wisdom and of revelation in the knowledge of him." Wisdom was a prominent subject in the Old

Testament (Prov. 1:1-7). To the Greeks, who prized wisdom, Paul presented Christ as the "wisdom of God" (1 Cor. 1:19-24). As a quality of the Christian life, wisdom does not mean having information or being clever. It means knowing God in humility and knowing how to live. Such wisdom comes by revelation. God, not man, is its source. It is in Christ that persons come to know God and to know how they are to live for him.

Such knowledge takes place in the believer as the eyes of his heart are enlightened. In biblical usage the heart is the center of will and understanding more than emotion. The physical eyes see physical objects and the heart sees spiritual realities. This prayer, then, asks for spiritual understanding.

Three objects of knowledge are specified. They needed to know that God had called them to a great hope. Throughout Ephesians the Christian life was described as a calling (4:1). Here it is "his calling." This means it originated with God, and he was active in urging persons to take part in it. It also suggests that it is dynamic, moving toward God's purpose. This goal of our calling provides hope. He has not only called us in the past and brought us to the present moment; he will lead us on to his ultimate goal for us. "Hope" in the Bible means much more than it does in modern speech. People today say "I hope" when they wish for something but are not sure it will happen. In the New Testament, hope means the confident expectation that something will happen. It is a joyous assurance, not just wishful thinking.

Paul also wanted the Ephesians to realize the quality and the extent of the blessings they had in Christ, "the riches of his glorious inheritance." Paul had already described the blessings of the Spirit as an inheritance (1:14). This image is found throughout the Bible. It stresses the fact that these blessings are received as a gift and that they are already guaranteed to us in the present even though they are not yet fully bestowed. The inheritance which the Christian awaits is rich both in quantity and quality.

The third object of knowledge desired is an understanding and experience of the power of God. God is at work in the life of a Christian in a powerful way. This power is "immeasurable." It is unlimited, and man cannot understand it. In addition to this adjective, Paul piled up four synonyms for strength in verse 19: power, working, might, and strength. The first two are Greek words which have formed our

English words "dynamic" and "energy." The last two words are combined in the Revised Standard Version as "great might." The total effect is to strain the limits of language to suggest something that cannot be put into words.

What God has done in Christ (1:20-23).—The mention of God's great power in verse 19 led Paul to talk about the greatest demonstration of that power, the resurrection. The Old Testament writers spoke of the Exodus from Egypt and the creation of the world when they wanted to show how powerful God was. The New Testament writers pointed to the resurrection. In Philippians 3:10 Paul included "the power of his resurrection" in his own prayer for increased knowledge of Christ. As the cross is the proof of the love of God, so the resurrection is the proof of his power.

In the New Testament the resurrection is always described with God as subject and Christ as object. It is an act of the Father toward the Son. Not only has God raised him from the dead; he has also enthroned him at his right hand, meaning the position of greatest honor and authority. The scene of his enthronement was also described as "in the heavenly places," the same term used in 1:3 for the scene of the Christian's blessings in Christ. The term here may have more of a sense of heaven as a place, but it still refers to the spiritual realm where God is at work in the lives of his people. This exaltation of Christ has put him above all other powers, real or imagined, which threaten men's lives.

Ancient people, especially the Gnostics, thought of a whole range of spiritual beings from lower to higher who affected human life. The Bible speaks of spiritual powers, both angels and demons, which are at work in the universe. This is the meaning of rule, authority, power, and dominion. Rule and authority are the same words translated "principalities" and "powers" in 6:12, references clearly applying to evil powers.

Paul's point here was that whatever powers there are, Christ is above them. The same went for "every name that is named"—that is, all the pagan gods by whatever name. God has put all the powers in existence under the feet of Christ (Ps. 8:6), under his power and authority. Christ is the head of all things. Even though he has not yet exercised his power to bring all things under his control (Heb. 2:8-9), he has that power; and in the church it is already experienced by his people.

This was the first use of the word "church" in Ephesians. It was a prominent theme in this letter. Here it was the arena in which the resurrection power of Christ over all things was experienced. The word for church means "called-out ones." In the ancient Greek translation of the Old Testament it was used to translate the word for the assembly of the people of Israel. In the New Testament it basically means a congregation of Christians. Sometimes, and especially in Ephesians, it takes on the larger meaning of all who are in Christ. This is the church in the general sense, sometimes called the universal church. In either sense of the word, local or universal, Christ is the head of the church.

This not only means that he is the church's authority and guide; it also means that he and his church exist in an organic unity. The church is "the fulness of him who fills all in all." This seems to mean that Christ fills everything, and God wants the church to be the full expression of Christ. There are other possible ways of translating this verse, including the possibility that it is Christ, not the church, who is the fullness of God, the one who fills all things. Some interpreters also suggest that this means the church in some way completes the fullness of Christ by making Christ effective in the world. However, such an idea is not supported by other New Testament statements.

From Death to Life (2:1-10)

Paul had mentioned the church, and he would return to this theme later. Now, however, he turned to describe the work of Christ in the lives of his people which enabled them to take part in the new people of God. Verses 1-10 are one long sentence in the original. They bring together in one statement all of Paul's teachings about sin, grace, faith, and the Christian life.

Dead in sin (2:1-3).—The verb in this passage, "made alive," does not come until verse 5. The King James Version and the Revised Standard Version anticipate for clarity by using it in verse 1. Those who are alive in Christ have not always been so. Looking back on their former lives, they see that they did not have life at all. Spiritually speaking, they were dead. Their existence was marked by "trespasses and sins." These words are close synonyms with different backgrounds. "Trespasses" is a word which indicated wrong steps or deliberate breaking of the law. "Sins" meant missing the mark. Together they continue the pattern of this epistle, emphasis by means of repetition.

These sins were not merely isolated acts; they were a way of life or pattern of conduct in which people had walked. The New Testament writers used vivid picture language instead of vague general terms. Life is a walk, an active process that moves along step by step.

This deadly walk was brought about by several factors. First, it was the way the world was going. "Course" in verse 2 is literally "age." This term and "world" are used throughout the New Testament to describe this present world order. The world as God created it and loves it (John 3:16) is good. But the world as sin has twisted it is a continuous evil influence on the people who live in it. The pressures of surrounding society lead them to walk away from God. But there are even more powerful forces at work. There is a superhuman, spiritual power of evil which generates a spirit of disobedience in people. Here he is called "the prince" or ruler of "the power of the air"—that is, the spiritual realm. Those who are influenced by him are called "sons of disobedience," a Hebrew way of saying "disobedient sons."

The mention of disobedience shows that it was man's own choice, not just the effect of Satan and the world, that made him go wrong. "The passions of our flesh" played an important part. These are the desires that come from man's lower nature. "Flesh" for Paul was not just the physical body but the whole personality apart from the control of the Spirit. To emphasize this, he went on to specify "the desires of body and mind." This pervasive tendency to evil shows that men are "by nature children of wrath." "Wrath" for Paul meant God's abiding opposition to evil and the destructive results of evil in human life. "By nature" does not mean that man's nature is basically evil but that what man naturally does in his fallen state is evil.

Throughout this passage it is stressed that "we all once lived [this way]" and are therefore "like the rest of mankind." What Paul has described is in some way true of every person, Jew or Gentile.

The riches of God's grace (2:4-7).—Against the dark background of spiritual death just described, verse 4 shines like the sun against the early morning sky. Hopelessness disappears with two little words, "But God!" If things were up to man there would be only death, but God has intervened. He has shown himself to be rich in mercy and not only a God of wrath. This mercy arises out of his love. It is not due to any deserving on man's part. On the contrary, it is in spite of sin and spiritual death.

Specifically, God's mercy has been shown in what he did in Christ. Not only did he provide forgiveness of sin through his death (1:7); he also gave new life by his resurrection. He has "made us alive together with Christ." Paul expressed this by putting a preposition meaning "with" on the front of the verb. God has coresurrected us with Christ. What happened to Christ can happen to us if we enter into union with him by faith. This thought of union with Christ, coupled with the mention of God's goodness, led Paul to insert in parentheses: "By grace you have been saved." He would go on to say more about this in verse 8.

At this point Paul stayed with the image of Christ in his resurrection, ascension, and enthronement. God has included the believer in all of this. He is brought to life from a state of death. He is raised to the presence of God and is seated in "the heavenly places," meaning the spiritual realm. These things may await complete fulfillment in the resurrection of the body at the end of time, but spiritually they have already happened. Those who are in Christ by faith share in his fellowship with God already.

What has already happened in the life of the believer does not exhaust the grace of God. The future is brighter still. God wants to "show the immeasurable riches of his grace" by his continuing kindness toward his people. "Kindness" is a word which means love in action. It is not clear whether "the coming ages" means the future course of history in this world or the new age beyond the end of the world. In the context of Ephesians it seems best to take it in the sense of experience in this world. God has saved his people for a purpose which he will continue to pursue throughout all time. He will always be lavishing his grace on them through Christ.

Saved through faith (2:8-10).—This passage is one of the best summaries of the gospel message in the New Testament. It contains key themes which Paul developed elsewhere and expresses them in a new way which would communicate to a wide audience in the Gentile world. For several verses Paul had been describing the riches of God's grace. In verse 5 he anticipated what he now wanted to say. Christians have received all the benefits of salvation as they have accepted the grace of God through their own response of faith.

"Grace" occurs twelve times in Ephesians. It was a word dear to Paul's heart. The early Christians took this word which had meant pleasantness, favor, or gratitude, and gave it new significance. As they

and later Christians used it, it described the utter generosity of God
which he gives to sinners even though they do not deserve it. This
grace is not only forgiveness of their sins but the gift of God's power
in their lives to enable a new kind of life.

"Saved" was used here to include all the various aspects of redemption. The word "saved" is in the past perfect tense. This means that
it is something accomplished in the past which continues to have
results in the present. Paul usually spoke of justification, reconciliation,
or adoption. "Saved" would be more easily understood by Gentiles
and served as a general term to include these other concepts.

"Faith" was also a favorite word of Paul's. It means much more
than agreeing with an idea. It means a total openness to let God
give the benefits of salvation and to obey the will of God. This does
not mean that faith is something man does by his own ability. It is
man's willingness to let God work in his life. It includes both trust
and commitment. Some think that "that not of yourselves" (KJV) refers
to faith and means that even our faith is God's gift. While this is
true in a sense, it is probably more accurate to take the phrase with
"saved."

Paul especially wanted to emphasize that this salvation was not
due to "works," what men can do. In Galatians and Romans he spelled
this out in terms of "works of the law." Here he was saying that
works of any kind are ineffective for salvation. The works approach
to salvation gives man some hope that he can boast or take credit
for his salvation. This is ruled out when salvation is totally dependent
on the grace of God. The Christian's whole life is a work of God.
Paul said, "We are his workmanship," a word from which we get
our English word "poem." The life of his people is God's work of
art.

Having said that works do not win salvation, Paul went on to affirm
that they do express salvation. God's plan for his people includes a
"walk," or course of living, that expresses itself in deeds of righteousness.

Unity in Christ (2:11-22)

Gentiles without hope (2:11-12).—"Therefore" indicates a transition at this point. Paul had been speaking of the blessings God gives
to the Christian. The emphasis had been on what Christians as individuals had received in Christ. Now he began to point to Christians as

a group. He reminded his Gentile readers that they were formerly
not a part of the people of God, but now in Christ they were. This
fact in itself was evidence of the greatness of God's working. As Gentiles, they were labeled "the uncircumcision" by the Jews. A physical
sign of obedience to the covenant symbolized the fact that they had
no part in the covenants God had made with Israel through Abraham,
Moses, and David. They were thus separated from Christ in the sense
that the Jews had the promise of the Messiah (the Hebrew term for
which "Christ" is the Greek), and the Gentiles did not. God's dealings
were with the nation of Israel, a nation to which the Gentiles were
aliens. Thus they had no hope. They were without God, a term from
which the word "atheist" is taken, even though the pagans had many
gods.

Christ reconciles all (2:13-18).—Just as Paul introduced the contrast
of life with death by the expression "but God" in verse 4, he introduced
another contrast in verse 13 with "but now in Christ Jesus." Those
who had been far removed from the people of God "have been
brought near." Those who had been separated from Christ, the Jewish
Messiah, were now in Christ Jesus, the one who had fulfilled the promise of the Messiah. The contrast between far off and near was drawn
from Isaiah 57:19. Believing Gentiles were now included in the family
of God. Gentiles who are in Christ are one with Jews who are in
Christ. This has been made possible by "the blood of Christ," meaning
the death of Christ on the cross (see on 1:7).

This joining of two previously separate groups was a great example
of "peace." It was Christ himself who created this peace. The word
"he" is emphatic, as if to say "he and he alone." He made the two
antagonistic peoples "one"—that is, a unity. In so doing he "has broken
down the dividing wall of hostility." This is a vivid figure of speech
for the spiritual barrier that had separated God from man as well
as the barrier that separated Jew from Gentile. Walls are notorious
dividers as seen in the infamous Berlin Wall that separates the Com-
munist East and the free West. But this is more than a figure of speech,
for there was an actual wall in the Temple in Jerusalem which separated Gentiles and Jews. The Gentiles were permitted to come into
the Court of the Gentiles, but signs carved in stone forbade them
to go further under penalty of death.

Christ did away with this barrier specifically "by abolishing in his
flesh the law of commandments and ordinances." These three words

may simply be emphatic repetition, or they may mean that the law
consisted of commandments which were expressed in more specific
ordinances or regulations. The heart of the law was its great moral
and spiritual principles. These Jesus approved and fulfilled, giving
them a new basis of spirit and love instead of legal requirements.
But the law also contained many ritual rules concerning diet, the
sabbath, circumcision, and purification. These Jesus abolished as no
longer necessary. These regulations had separated Jew and Gentile.
They need do so no longer. "In his flesh" may mean in his death on
the cross, or it may mean in his life and ministry.

Christ's work of abolishing separation aimed at nothing less than
the creation of "one new man." There was no longer Jew and Gentile
in Christ. Now there was only Christian. In this way, by an act of
new creation, he has made peace.

Both Jew and Gentile had been reconciled to God through Christ.
They had also been reconciled to one another. Thus they were in
one body, and that body was at peace with God. As in verse 13, so
in verse 16, this reconciliation was made possible by the death of
Christ on the cross or by his blood. By taking on himself the judgment
for sin and the effects of man's hostility to God, Christ absorbed and
overcame all that separates persons from God and from each other.

Not only did Jesus accomplish this reconciliation; he also launched
a mission of preaching it to those who were near (the Jews) and to
those who were far off (the Gentiles). Commentators disagree as to
whether "he came and preached" referred to the earthly ministry
of Jesus, his resurrection appearances, or the mission of his followers.
Perhaps the entire spectrum of Christian proclamation was intended.
In whatever way, Jesus brings the message of peace. As the result
of all he has done, all persons, both Jew and Gentile, have access to
God. They come through the same Spirit, and by this Spirit they
are able to relate to God as Father.

A holy temple (2:19-22).—The Gentiles had been strangers and
sojourners, the latter word meaning a resident alien, one who lived
in one territory but was a citizen of another. Now, however, they
were citizens too. Not only that, but they were members of the family,
"the household of God." The image, having shifted from citizenship
to household, now shifted again to a building, a temple. God's people
were to be a structure where God could dwell with them in fellowship,

the basic meaning of the temple. Such a place was built up in the Spirit out of the lives of people.

At the base of the structure were the apostles and prophets, the earliest witnesses to the Christ event. The apostles were those eyewitnesses appointed by Christ to declare his message (see 1:1). The prophets were inspired persons in the early church who interpreted the mind of Christ for the situation of their day (see 3:5; 4:11). By mentioning them as the foundation, Paul was stressing the historical link that bound the church to its source. This source, Christ himself, was called "the cornerstone." He was the very first stone in place, the one which gave all the others their true places. Thus the Gentiles, along with the Jews, were part of a spiritual structure which was really a living body. In them God dwelt with men.

The Stewardship of the Mystery (3:1-6)

Reflecting on the vision of Jew and Gentile together in Christ, Paul was moved once again to prayer and praise. He seemed about to voice a prayer as he did in 1:15, where the phrase "For this reason" was also used in this way. In doing so, he identified himself as the one who had given himself for the sake of the Gentiles, even to the point of being in prison. This showed how deeply he felt about God's plan to unite Jew and Gentile in Christ.

Having digressed from his prayer impulse to make this point, Paul began to elaborate on it further. He actually did not return to his prayer until verse 14, where he repeated the introductory phrase, "For this reason." He wanted to be sure his readers knew the special role God had given him in the mission to the Gentiles and the special nature of his message. If the epistle were written only to the Ephesians this statement would not be necessary, for they knew Paul very well. But since it was a general letter to the Gentile Christians, some would need more background information.

The point was that Paul had been given a "stewardship," the same word translated "plan" in 1:10. The concept of the Christian as a steward was common in the New Testament. The steward was the household manager who was entrusted by the master of the house with the responsibility of taking care of things for him. The grace of God which Paul had described at such length in this letter was given to him in just this way. God trusted him with this message for the specific purpose of delivering it to the Gentiles and including them in the people of God.

As Paul had already written earlier in the letter (1:9), the inclusion of the Gentiles was a mystery, something which no one could have foreseen. But the secret was now an open secret because God had revealed it to Paul in his conversion and call to missions. He had an insight into "the mystery of Christ." It was the theme of his ministry. It was not known to the men of former times, but it had been revealed by the Spirit, not only to Paul but to all of the apostles and prophets on whom the new people of God were built (2:20).

Verse 6 sums up the mystery once again: It was the wonderful way in which the Gentiles had been included in Christ through the preaching of the good news. They were "fellow heirs." They, along with the Jews, received the inheritance which God promised to his people beginning with Abraham. They, too, were God's children. They were "members of the same body." There was only one people of God. In the church, through Christ, all believers take part in it regardless of human differences. They are "partakers of the promise." In Christ God had fulfilled his promises to his people, and the Gentile Christians are full-fledged recipients along with Jewish Christians.

Made a Minister (3:7-13)

The good news mentioned in verse 6 was the focus of Paul's ministry. This ministry was not something he chose. Rather, he was "made a minister," literally a "deacon," meaning a servant. It was not his own accomplishment, for his whole life was going in the opposite direction as he persecuted the church and trusted in the law. Rather, his appointment as a minister was a "gift of God's grace." And not only did God have to show mercy to him to make him a minister; he also had to provide the power. And this power was not something provided from a distance. It was something that worked in Paul's life, literally "the energizing or inworking of his dynamic." All of this God did in Paul's life although he was "the very least of all the saints." This was not just false modesty on Paul's part. Those saints who are closest to God invariably have a strong sense of their own unworthiness. And Paul was acutely aware that he had previously been an active enemy of God's people.

God's grace had been given to him, Paul said, for one great purpose: "to preach to the Gentiles the unsearchable riches of Christ." He was fond of describing the blessings of Christ in terms of wealth (Eph. 1:18; 2 Cor. 8:9). Here he added the descriptive word "unsearchable." This word came from the Greek word meaning "to track out" and with the negative prefix means "untrackable." It is so vast no explorer can explore it, so deep no line can plumb its depths.

Because of the generosity of God's grace and the nature of his commission, Paul wanted "to make all men see" the great thing God was doing. As he had already done in this book, he described the divine enterprise as "the plan of the mystery hidden for ages." "Plan" was the same word used in 1:10. The source and repository of this plan had been God. What had happened in Christ was the plan of none other than the Creator himself. Creation and redemption are part of the one master plan in the mind of God.

The arena in which this plan had been unfolded was the church. It was the practical laboratory in which God's work of redeeming and unifying took place. Here the wisdom of God was seen to be "manifold" or, better, "richly diversified." As a result of this revealing process going on through the church, God's plan had become known "to the principalities and powers in the heavenly places." The evil powers which were at work in the spiritual realm could not know of God's wise and wonderful plan until they saw what was happening in the church. Now even they knew that God had a plan that would undo all their work to divide mankind.

All of this had happened through God's plan, and the plan had been "realized" or put into effect through Christ, whom Paul described as "our Lord." In him the universal plan became a personal experience. Rather than being overwhelmed by the greatness and power of God's magnificent plan, the believer in Christ finds himself in a close personal relationship with God. Christ gives him the boldness and confidence to come to God in faith.

On this basis the apostle reassured his friends. He was in prison, suffering for their sake. This could be distressing to them, but he urged them not to lose heart. By their acceptance of his suffering and by their life as God's church, they demonstrated the glory Paul had been talking about.

Prayer and Praise (3:14-21)

Intercession (3:14-19).—Having explained his role in carrying the message of God's great plan, Paul now returned to the prayer he was about to express in verse 1. He repeated the phrase "For this reason," which referred to all he had said in the first two chapters. This vision of God's grace and the blessings of Christ moved him to humility and prayer. He bowed his knees before God. The usual Jewish position for prayer was standing. Kneeling was the posture of homage or submission and was also used in prayer as in Daniel 6:10 and Acts 7:59-60. The passage that follows here is obviously a prayer and one that is rich in wonder at the blessings of God both past and future.

God was identified as "the Father from whom every family in heaven and on earth is named." This again relates God to the church in which all believers, both Jew and Gentile, are united. The two words "Father" and "family" are variations of the same root word in Greek. They could be literally translated "Father" and "father-group." This may refer to the fact that human fatherhood was patterned after divine fatherhood, but it is more likely that it referred to the churches as families that belong in the one great family of God the Father.

As the basis of his prayer for his readers, Paul again referred to the riches of God. "Riches of his glory" could be translated "glorious riches." These are the vast resources out of which God can supply all the needs of his people and on which they draw in prayer. Having defined this resource, Paul went on to ask for several blessings from this rich store to be given to the readers. The focus of the prayer was on the inner life of believers in their personal relation to God.

The first request was for inner strength. He prayed that they might be made strong as God's power worked in them. "The inner man" was the person as he really was in the center of his life. It is here, and not in some outer defense, that real strength lies. Such strength comes through the Spirit, meaning God as he is present and active in the Christian's life. The strength God gives is himself. This was also seen in the second request, "that Christ may dwell in your hearts through faith." The presence of God in the believer's life is sometimes thought of as the Holy Spirit and sometimes as the indwelling Christ. The two are inseparably linked, just as all three persons of the Trinity are in Christian doctrine. What one does the others are involved in, for the three are one.

The prayer now shifts focus to the response and outlook of the Christian. It is "through faith" that Christ dwells in one's life. No ritual or organization can bring this about. It must be appropriated by personal trust and commitment. Faith is linked with love as in 1:15. Having a new inner strength and experiencing the presence of Christ, the believer also has a new orientation to others. Love is the foundation of his life. *The New English Bible* translates "rooted and grounded" as "with deep roots and firm foundations."

In verses 18 and 19 the emphasis is on spiritual understanding as it was in the earlier prayer in 1:15-23. Paul wanted his readers to share in something that is experienced by all the saints, all the people of God. That is a "power to comprehend" the love of Christ. (Though love was not specified in verse 18, it was clearly in Paul's mind in vv. 17,19.) The love of Christ is so vast that Paul suggested its dimensions as "breadth and length and height and depth." These are not specific elements to be analyzed but are designed to show the all-embracing scope of Christ's love.

Paul said that the love of Christ "surpasses knowledge," yet he prayed that they might know it. Clearly he meant much more than intellectual knowledge, but he did mean to say that in Christ Christians somehow know the unknowable. The ultimate goal of the prayer was that Christians "may be filled with all the fullness of God." God's purpose is to dwell with his people, and the Christian life is a process of growth to this end. The fullness of God seems to mean all that God means for us to have.

Doxology (3:20-21).—The letter reached a climax at this point. Here the affirmation of great truths and the listing of great blessings came to an end. The last half of the book would turn to an appeal for worthy living. The first section closed with a beautiful exclamation of praise to God. "Now to him who . . . is able" is a common formula of praise (Rom. 16:25). God was praised for the "power at work in us," an emphasis made several times in these three chapters. Another repeated emphasis was on the lavish abundance of God's blessings. Here the term "far more" was a very emphatic phrase that meant "far, far more." God's ability to work in his people was more than they could ever imagine or ask for.

Such great power and grace called for glory to be given to God. This is to take place in the church, once more the scene of the unfolding of God's purpose. Paul added "in Christ" in a way that is hard to interpret. Perhaps it referred to the fact that what happens in the church happens in Christ. Certainly he taught that the unfolding of God's purpose which reveals his glory takes place in Christ. This glorifying of God in the life of the church was to continue for all time and throughout eternity. A magnificent vision, to which Paul aptly said, "Amen."

Worthy Living for God's People

4:1 to 6:24

The Unity and Purpose of the Church (4:1-16)

A worthy life (4:1-3)—Doctrines cannot be separated from deeds. Paul's writings always touch real life, and Ephesians is no exception. As in his other letters, the first half of the book discusses the great truths of redemption and the last half spells out practical ways of responding to these truths. This is the pattern, for example in Colossians and 1 Thessalonians. In Romans 12:1, the transitional statement is just like this one: "I appeal to you therefore, brethren." The word "therefore" points back to the great affirmations of the early chapters and forward to the great exhortations of the closing chapters.

Paul strengthened his appeal by identifying himself as "a prisoner for the Lord." He had responded to God's grace with a dedication that had brought him to prison. But the real tie that held him was not chains and bars. It was the claim of Christ on his life.

The word "beg" does not do justice to the word Paul used, which means "exhort" or "beseech." The thing he asked of them summarizes all that he would say in the next three chapters. He wanted them to "lead a life," literally "walk," that will do justice to the glorious calling of God in their lives. Questions of behavior are to be resolved by asking, "Will this act express and honor the great mission in life that God has given me?" Christians have been called to "sit with him in the heavenly places" (2:6). Their daily lives must reflect this.

The description of the Christian life as a calling means that it is much more than a gift or a privilege. A calling comes from someone who has the right to claim our loyalty. It leads in the direction of a purpose beyond ourselves. It means that Christian living is goal-oriented and dynamic. The way Paul used the word here also shows that it is not only the apostles and missionaries who are called, but all Christians. The calling is not just to a certain vocation or mission; it is to a way of life.

This way of life is defined here in terms of definite attitudes and actions. The same four virtues are listed which appear in Colossians 3:12. Two of them, meekness and patience, are listed with the fruit of the Spirit in Galatians 5:22 (see the comments on this passage). The term "lowliness" was coined by Christians to describe humility. It contains a Greek adjective that meant slavish or cringing. The ancients did not have a word for humility that was not degrading. They did not consider it a virtue. But for those who follow Christ, it takes on a new meaning and becomes one of the chief virtues. Christians took the best words available to express new realities and put meaning into them with their lives. "Meekness," another word for humility, means mildness or gentleness and is used of an animal that had been tamed. Thus it suggests controlled strength, not weakness. Moses was meek, according to Numbers 12:3; but he was certainly not weak.

"Longsuffering" means endurance and is one of the major Christian qualities. It is the attitude God has toward humanity (Rom. 2:4, which also includes "forbearance") and the attitude Christians also show toward others and toward suffering. "Forbearing one another" is the practical expression of longsuffering. It involves accepting the weaknesses of others and loving them in spite of their faults. "Love" is the background of all these qualities. This is the way people live who are "rooted and grounded in love" (3:17).

All of these qualities are related to a matter Paul wanted to deal with at some length, the unity of the church. Christians are to exercise these virtues because they are "eager to maintain" this unity. The word translated "eager" is quite strong. *The New English Bible* translates it "spare no effort." Obviously this is a high-priority concern. Such unity is "of the spirit." It is not possible on merely human terms. It is a product of the working of the Holy Spirit in the lives of God's people. They are to keep this unity by living in a relationship of peace with one another.

All in one (4:4-6).—Paul now listed the great spiritual realities that unite all Christians. This is a kind of checklist of things believers everywhere should be able to agree on, even though they will differ on many secondary points. The first one is that "there is one body." The church is the body of Christ (1:23). With Christ as its head, the body cannot be divided. It is unthinkable that there could be more than one body of Christ, even though that one body has many local manifestations. The idea of the body of Christ expresses a spiritual reality, but it also includes the idea of an actual body of people who demonstrate the life of Christ in the world. Christians should work to achieve unity with other Christians, in every way short of compromise, on primary truths and values. Paul specifically has in mind here that Gentiles and Jews who are in Christ must realize that they are part of one and the same body.

There is also "one Spirit," meaning the Holy Spirit. At the most basic level, the thing that unites a group of Christians is that in each of them the same power and person is at work. Paul makes it clear that anyone who has received Christ has received the Holy Spirit (1:13). This greatest fact of his life is something he has in common with every other Christian. It is also significant that this list of great unities includes all three persons of the Trinity.

Mention of the Spirit leads to an affirmation of hope, as it did in 1:13-14. All Christians share in the call of God to his great purpose. They all look forward to the same great future. They all pursue the same goal.

At the heart of Christian experience and faith is Christ, the "one Lord." Just as all the spokes of a wheel are held together and properly arranged by their relation to the common hub, so all Christians come together around the one Lord. Two people who are both loyal to Christ cannot be opposed to one another. The "one faith" is the common commitment that believers have to the one Lord. This original meaning of faith as personal trust and commitment gradually came to extend to faith as a body of truths which are believed. It is possible that this meaning is intended here. The one faith is expressed outwardly and visibly in "one baptism." Baptism is the sign of beginning the Christian life which all Christians share, even though there has come to be much disagreement about the form and meaning of the act.

Finally, and most basic of all, there is "one God and Father of us all." The ultimate basis of all unity is the oneness of God. If there were many Gods, the world would be hopelessly divided among them; but there is only one. All people, whatever their race, color, or national origin, are created by the same Creator. Paul said that God is above all and through all and in all. This means that God is supreme and transcendent. He is also active in all people and in all that happens.

Building up the body of Christ (4:7-16).—Having stressed unity, Paul now turned to think of the diversity that exists in the body of Christ. This is the reason the sentence begins with "But." God has given his grace to each believer. He has not been stingy in doing this. "The measure of Christ's gift" suggests that he does not hold anything back (see Rom. 8:32). The idea of measure may also suggest that the gift is individually tailored to each Christian.

To further develop the idea of Christ giving gifts to his church, Paul cited Psalm 68:18, which describes God returning in triumph after the defeat of the enemies of his people. As returning conquerors usually did in the ancient world, he led a parade of captives as he returned. The original Hebrew psalm then says "receiving gifts among men." Paul gave this phrase as "he gave gifts to men." There is some evidence to show that Jewish writers before Paul quoted the verse with this variation. Some Christian interpreters have felt that Paul had the authority as an inspired writer and apostle to make the change himself. In either case, the point here is that Christ has ascended as the conquerer of sin and death, and out of his wealth he has given gifts to his people.

Paul further explained that the reference to Christ's ascending implies that he had first descended. This descent seems to correspond to his emptying himself and coming in the flesh to dwell among men and to die (Phil. 2:5-11; John 1:1-18). Two other interpretations of the verse are sometimes proposed. Some think the descent was what was described in 1 Peter 3:19 and refers to a visit to the realm of the dead between Christ's death and resurrection. Others suggest that this descent was the coming of the Holy Spirit at Pentecost. Paul emphasized the fact that the one who ascended was the same as the one who descended. This seems to be aimed at early false teachers who said that the glorified Christ could not have experienced real human life and death. The impact of this passage is that Christ, by his incarnation, death, resurrection, and ascension has become available to "fill all things." He is able to give to his people all that is needed to fulfill their calling.

In verse 11 Christ's gifts to his people are named. In general terms his gift to his people is the Holy Spirit (Acts 1:8). But the Spirit himself is said to give a variety of gifts. Here the gifts are specified in terms of functions which are performed in the church and persons who perform those functions.

First there are "apostles." The apostles were the original witnesses of Christ's life, death, and resurrection. Their function was to give a true presentation of the gospel and to launch the missionary movement. The word means "sent ones" (see comments on 2 Cor. 1:1 and Gal. 1:1).

"Prophets" were persons who were recognized as speaking with authority. Their words were especially important before the New Testament writings became available to the churches to interpret the will of God. They were able to speak the word of God in special situations to foretell (Acts 11:28; 21:9,11), to convict (1 Cor. 14:24-25), and to encourage (Acts 15:32).

"Evangelists" were Christians who had the ability to communicate the gospel to persons outside the church, those we ordinarily call missionaries today. Philip is called an evangelist in Acts 21:8, and Timothy is encouraged to work as an evangelist in 2 Timothy 4:5.

"Pastors" is the translation of a word that means "shepherds." The word "some" is repeated for each individual term up to this point, but "pastors and teachers" are linked together with one use of the word "some." The two are inseparably linked. Pastors are to care for the flock of God, feeding and protecting them. Teachers are to instruct. One person may do both. Some may specialize or emphasize one more than the other. But the church needs both.

All of these persons and functions aim at one purpose described in verse 12. It is expressed in three phrases which are variously grouped by different translators and interpreters. The original edition of the Revised Standard Version (1946) follows the King James Version and puts the comma after saints. Thus there are three purposes: "for the equipment of the saints, for the work of ministry, for building up the body of Christ." The second edition of the Revised Standard Version (1971) takes the first two phrases together, leaving out the comma: "to equip the saints for the work of ministry, for building up the body of Christ." As there are no commas in the early Greek manuscripts, placing one here is a matter of interpretation. The grammar favors the later translation, as do most recent commentators. The New English Bible has "to equip God's people for work in his service, to the building up of the body of Christ." In this translation, the work of ministry is to be done by all of God's people. The special workers in the church are to equip the people to carry out their ministry. Equippers and lay ministers all aim at building up the church.

"To equip" translates a noun which is found only here in the New

Testament. The verb form is used in Matthew 4:21 to describe mending nets and in Galatians 6:1 to refer to restoring Christians to spiritual health. In Hebrews 11:3 it is used of the creation of the universe. The word here has no sense of restoring from a fallen or broken state. It means bringing God's people to a condition in which they are fit to accomplish God's purpose.

"The saints" who are to be equipped are all of God's people (see comments on 1:1). The "work of ministry" is simply service, the word which also means deaconship (see comments on 3:7). What Paul means by "building up the body of Christ" will be seen in verses 13-16.

Paul has in mind a process that moves toward the goal of Christlikeness. "Attain" is a word used in Acts for travelers arriving at their destination. One part of the goal is unity. This has been emphasized in verses 3-6. It is unity that grows out of the common faith believers share. Another way of saying this is that it is unity that comes from knowing the Son of God. Paul usually refers to Jesus as Christ and Lord, but when he wants to stress the unique nature of Jesus he sometimes speaks of him as "Son of God" (Rom. 1:4; Gal. 2:20; 1 Thess. 1:10). By knowing Christ in the deepest possible way, believers experience him as the one who shows God's character and brings God's presence as no one else does. This revolutionary knowledge binds Christians together in unity.

Another way of describing the goal of the church's life is "mature manhood." "Mature" is a word which can also be translated "perfect," as in the King James Version. It has the idea of being complete or reaching the goal. For the church to reach its goal, it must have in its membership persons who are individually attaining God's will for their lives. This kind of maturity is necessary if there is to be unity in the church. It is the opposite of the instability described in verse 14.

The meaning of this maturity is found in the next phrase, "to the measure of the stature of the fullness of Christ." A complete person is one who measures up to the pattern of personhood displayed by Christ. This means much more than merely human definitions of maturity. The fullness of Christ here seems to mean all that Christ wants in the lives of his people.

The alternative to Christian maturity is a childish tendency to be carried away by false teachings and unscrupulous leaders. Children are fascinated by something new and do not have the ability to judge the value of things without their elders' help. In spiritual matters, even adults can be children, and novel religious teachings continue to win followers. Paul described such people as a boat, swept away and whirled around by the wind. He warned of people who are eager to do this. They use "cunning," literally "playing with dice" or "trickery"; "cleverness," literally "every deed"; and " deceitful wiles," literally "following a wandering way." Those who want to can find many ways of manipulating the immature. All of this is the very opposite of the way Christ wants the church to be.

Instead of such falsehood and manipulation, mature Christians are characterized by truth and love. "Speaking the truth" means also doing the truth (there is no word for speaking in the text). Christ is the truth (John 14:6), and God's people must be loyal to the truth in all they say and do. This must be done with love. People are as important as principles, and the truth must be practiced with kindness and helpfulness. Truth without love is fanaticism. Love without truth is sentimentality. By holding both in balance, Christians grow to be like Christ in definite steps of practical living. We should approach every situation in life by asking, "What will bring us closer to Christ and make us most like him?" In this way the church will be built up.

The focus now shifts from the church and its members to Christ as the head and the parts of the body working together. All the members with their various gifts depend on him. The effectiveness and growth of the body depends on all "working properly" together. Once again love is given as the means and the manner for building up the church.

Put on the New Nature (4:17-24)

Verse 17 begins with an urgent signal that says, "This is important!" Paul used words taken from the law court to emphasize the truth and seriousness of what he was about to say. He also pointed to his spiritual authority as one who was "in the Lord." The object of this special emphasis was a warning: "You must no longer live as the Gentiles do." They were, of course, Gentiles by birth. But now they had a new nature and a new identity. They were a part of the new Israel in Christ. Paul wanted to be sure they understood that this meant a new quality of life and new ways of behaving. Those Christians who had been Jews had the high moral standards of the Old Testament.

Gentiles, however, came from a pagan background without such clear guidance in morality. As Christians they needed thorough instruction in how to live the new life and encouragement to resist the pressures of their pagan surroundings.

The description that follows is very similar to the one in Romans 1:21-24. Without divine guidance, their way of thinking was futile. Life lacked a sense of meaning and purpose. Their understanding was dark. Darkness in the New Testament symbolizes evil and moral confusion. Such darkness meant that they could not tell right from wrong. Such a lack of ethical perception was a kind of ignorance, but it was more than a mental deficiency. They were actually separated from the life that God gives.

Moral living was not something extra for persons to do. It was the very content of eternal life. This moral ignorance was not a circumstance beyond their control; it was "due to their hardness of heart." This is a biblical phrase to describe the insensitivity to spiritual things that comes from persistent rejection of God (Rom. 11:7,25). Like hands that constantly handle rough objects, their hearts had become "callous"—that is, insensitive to the pain of conscience. They had given in or yielded themselves to "licentiousness" or unrestrained immorality, especially sexual misconduct. They greedily engaged in every kind of shameful conduct.

In verse 20 the direction of the discussion changed abruptly: "You did not so learn Christ!" They could not live in the shameful manner just described. Something had happened to them that totally eliminated any such possibility. They had "learned Christ." The use of "learned" to describe their experience of Christ was unusual. It was used in contrast to the lack of moral understanding in verses 17-18. It was similar to Jesus' call for people to "learn of me" (Matt. 11:29). It may have been intended to emphasize the teaching aspect of Christianity which was so important in the Gentile churches. The meaning is clarified by verse 21. To trigger a response from his readers, Paul posed an implied question as to whether they had in fact "heard about him and were taught in him, as the truth is in Jesus." Thus to learn Christ was to hear the facts about him, to be taught concerning him, and to receive the truth which is revealed in him.

Becoming a Christian was much more than learning truths with the mind. This was made clear in the next three verses (vv. 22-24). A complete break with past life was involved. The person who was

in Christ had taken off his old nature as a man takes off an old suit
he never wants to wear again.

This old nature was the source of the old way of life. The only
way to change the old behavior was to change the inner nature; and
once the inner nature had been changed, the outward behavior must
change too. The old nature must be changed because it has been
corrupted by evil desires that are deceitful. They promised happiness,
but they did not deliver. Instead they led to the shameful things
Paul had described in verses 18-19. Verse 23 shows that the change
is not just outward, as in the case of changing clothes. It really involves
being "renewed in the spirit of your minds." Just as when a man
leaves civilian life for the military, the outward change of uniform
reflects an inner change of identity and purpose.

The use of the present tense here suggests that inner spiritual re-
newal is a continuing process for the Christian. The image is completed
in verse 23. The Christian puts on a new nature. As in the creation
account of Genesis 1:27, he is "created after the likeness of God."
This likeness is described as "righteousness," right standing with God
and the right conduct that results, and "holiness," the quality that
belongs especially to God and so characterizes those who belong to
him.

Examples of the New Way of Life (4:25 to 5:2)

Speaking the truth (4:25).—Each of the examples of behavior in
this section gave the characteristic of the old nature that was rejected
and then stated a characteristic of the new nature that was to replace
it. It was not enough to stop doing evil. Christians must start doing
good. One of the negative items was "putting away" (the phrase used
in v. 25) falsehood. The virtue to be put on was to "speak the truth"
(already mentioned in v. 15). The wording of this counsel is taken
from Zechariah 8:16. The reason for this instruction is that "we are
members one of another." Christians depend on one another so much
that they must be able to trust the words and deeds of their fellow
believers. As the ancient preacher Chrysostom said, "If the eye sees
a serpent, does it deceive the foot? If the tongue tastes what is bitter,
does it deceive the stomach?"[1] The members of the body must be
able to trust one another.

Dealing with anger (4:26-27).—"Be angry but do not sin" is a quotation from Psalm 4:4. It is a Hebrew way of saying, "When you are

angry, do not sin." It is not blanket permission to be angry. Still, the way Paul used it does recognize that anger is a part of life and must be handled constructively. There is justifiable, righteous anger, such as Jesus showed toward the money changers in the Temple. But it is all too easy to let lower motives creep in and turn such anger to personal bitterness. There is also the normal conflict that constantly occurs between persons. If handled openly and lovingly, it can be worked through and laid to rest. It needs to be expressed in appropriate ways in order to be healed.

But it is all too easy to build up such negative feelings only to unload them on others in ways and at times that are not appropriate. This kind of anger keeps wounds open and perpetuates pain. Recognizing such potential danger, Paul urged Christians to settle before sundown. Clearing the emotional atmosphere and resolving the day's conflicts is a prescription for a good night's sleep and a peaceful tomorrow. As verse 27 indicates, failure to handle anger gives the devil just what he needs to get his foot in the door.

Honest work (4:28).—Among those who become Christians, there are some who had lived by dishonest means. How does such a person make the change to a new life? A thief, Paul said, will put away his stealing with the old nature he puts off. But he will have to replace the old habits with new habits if there is to be real change. The prescription for him is to "labor," a word that means strenuous, fatiguing work. The hands that used to steal must now do honest work. Paul himself had worked with his hands to avoid any suspicion of selfish gain in Corinth (1 Cor. 4:12). The motive for the new work habits must not be one's own profit. Besides meeting their own basic needs, Christians are to work so that they can give to others who are in need. The antidote for a habit of taking is to develop a habit of giving.

Gracious speech (4:29).—Becoming a Christian will even change the way a person talks. The old nature produces talk that is "evil," a word meaning rotten, as in the case of spoiled food. The context indicates that this does not just mean profanity or vulgar language. It is any kind of talk that tears down and lowers the moral level of the community. It is linked with slander in Colossians 3:8. The new nature will express itself in speech that has three characteristics. It edifies or builds up; it is appropriate, the right word at the right time; and it imparts grace. It has a redemptive effect on those who hear it and brings the most Godlike quality of all to the lives of others.

Harmony with the Spirit (4:30).—This verse does not follow the pattern of contrasting pairs of actions. It may be an introduction to the two sets of characteristics that follow, or it may stand alone in the midst of the list of contrasts. Paul at this point wanted to emphasize that the new nature in us is the work of the Spirit. To continue doing the things characteristic of the old nature would be a personal insult to the Spirit, who is God himself in the believer's life. The word "grieve" is very personal. God is saddened and disappointed when his people do not live up to their new nature. As in 1:13-14, the Spirit is the seal and guarantee of our future complete redemption.

Christlike relationships (4:31-32).—Following the warning against grieving the Spirit, Paul listed six forms of sin which are in sharp contrast to the influence of the Spirit and must be put away. They are sins which are usually expressed in speech, and they all involve relationships with others. "Bitterness" is the spirit of resentment that refuses to be reconciled. "Wrath" is an outburst of temper, while "anger" is a persistent antagonism against something or someone. "Clamor" is a loud expression of grievance, as when one shouts in the face of another. "Slander" is literally "blasphemy," which is used in the Bible for words spoken against men as well as against God. "All malice" is a general term which includes any kind of evil word or act against another.

The Christian is to put off all such things, and put on the opposite qualities. "Kind" is a word that describes love in action. Used by Jesus of his yoke, it is translated "easy" (Matt. 11:30). It describes that which fits comfortably. Thus a kind person is one who is considerate of others and strives to fit his actions to their needs. "Tenderhearted" means compassionate or sympathetic. To be specific, this means "forgiving one another," a general term for forgiveness which means "treating with grace." If people are to be united in one body and live as Christians, they must forgive each other. The model for such forgiveness is Christ himself. His people are to forgive in the same way he has forgiven them.

Imitators of God (5:1-2).—The chapter division at 5:1 obscures the connection with what has gone before. Paul had urged believers to put on a new nature because they had been "created after the likeness of God" (4:24). Now he summed up his argument by stating this truth in a bold and striking phrase, "Be imitators of God." Those who are

God's children are to be like their Father. He is the source of their new nature. In a more immediate, visible way the new nature is portrayed by Christ. Christians are to "walk in love," and the pattern for this way of life is the way Christ gave himself for them as a demonstration of his love. His death was "a fragrant offering," a Jewish term that means it was pleasing to God. It was a sacrifice. It did all that the sacrifices in the Temple were aimed at doing in atoning for sin.

Thus the death of Christ is the source of our ability to live new lives, and it is the pattern that shows how those new lives are to be lived. In Romans 12:1 the Christian's response to God's grace is compared to presenting "a living sacrifice." We are to give our lives to God in holy living just as Christ gave his life to God on the cross.

Further Warnings (5:3-14)

After the high point and summary statement in verses 1-2, Paul seemed to double back and attack again the sins of the pagan world. This indicates the urgency of the problem. We know from the rest of the New Testament that the rise of false teachings in the last part of the first century brought a new wave of immorality. Such heretics as the Gnostics taught that only the spiritual mattered. What was done with the physical body was not important. Christians, according to this view, had freedom to behave as they desired. Paul saw such tendencies as a lapse back into the old pagan immorality. In this section he was particularly concerned about sexual immorality. The focus is not on the deeds themselves but on the danger of even talking about them or associating with others who practiced them.

"Fornication" ("immorality" in the RSV, 1st ed.) comes from the Greek word from which we get pornography. It denotes sexual relations outside of marriage. "Impurity" is a broader term for immorality or uncleanness. "Covetousness" is a word for greed which was often used to denote uncontrolled sexual desire (see 4:19). Though Paul found it necessary to list them, he said that it was not appropriate for Christians even to talk about them. Those who become comfortable discussing such things and lose their capacity to be shocked by them are in danger of slipping from words to deeds. Also, the conversation of holy people should have a wholly different character.

Three other categories of conversation are also rejected. "Filthiness" means that which is shameful. "Silly talk" is the conversation of a fool or a drunkard. "Levity" is witty or clever talk that is improper.

Language that makes light of human weakness or human goodness ultimately tears down the quality of life. Instead of these, Paul said, "let there be thanksgiving." This word can mean "gracious speech," but the usual meaning is gratitude. Thanksgiving puts all conversation in perspective. It recalls that God is the source of good and places everything in relation to him. With such an outlook, speech is purified; and all of life becomes worship.

To underline the seriousness of immoral behavior, Paul stated that persons who practice these evils (the fornicator, the impure, and the covetous, as in v. 3) will not share in the inheritance of the kingdom of God. Here in verse 5 covetousness is linked with idolatry. Uncontrolled desire for anything is equivalent with making that thing your god. Such persons are excluded from the kingdom, not because these sins are worse than others but because any sin that controls a life means that life is not under God's control. Being under the control of God is what the kingdom is all about. A person cannot live for self or pleasure or material things and also live for the kingdom of God.

Verses 6-7 indicates that some taught differently. Like the later Gnostics, they said these things did not matter. Paul disagreed. These things result in the wrath of God on those who are disobedient to God. No matter how convincing the argument for such actions, it is composed of "empty words." God's people ought not even associate with those who advocate such a view.

Verses 8-14 are a graphic little sermon on light and darkness. These terms are often used in the New Testament to describe the contrast between righteousness and sin. Paul was saying that a return to immoral living would be a return to the state of moral and spiritual darkness of their former life. Not only did they live and walk in darkness; they were darkness. Their very nature was characterized by the absence of light. Now, in Christ, they were light.

Light, because it is the nature of Christ, produces fruit that is "good and right and true." Paul urged them to "walk"—that is, live and behave—"as children of light." Another way of saying this is, "Try to learn what is pleasing to the Lord." It is not necessary to spell out the details. The guiding rule is whether an attitude or action is pleasing to the Lord. Christians should avoid the "works of darkness" because they are "unfruitful." But they are also to be on the offensive.

They should "expose" the works of darkness, show them up for what they really are. This does not mean to talk about them, for they are too shameful to talk about. It means to show them up by living a better kind of life.

A life that is light will expose dark things; and when they are lighted up, they will begin to be influenced by the light. It is difficult to tell the precise meaning of verse 13. In some sense the thing that is exposed and becomes visible "is light." This may mean that it is shown up for what it is, or that it will become a means of witness to others, or that it will yield to the power of the light.

To conclude this thought, Paul introduced a quotation. It is similar to Isaiah 6:1, but it is not a direct quotation; and it includes the name of Christ. This has led most commentators to think that it is from an early Christian hymn, perhaps one connected with baptism. It describes the beginning of the Christian life as waking from sleep, as rising from the dead, and as receiving light. Clearly people who have experienced this cannot take part in the ways of sleep, death, and darkness.

The Walk of the Wise (5:15-20)

Paul continued his exhortation with a plea for a manner of life that is appropriate for such people at such a time. In the light of their redemption from darkness to light, they must take decisive steps. They must "look carefully," taking advantage of the light they have in a dark world. The way they walk is of critical importance. They must be wise with the wisdom prayed for earlier (1:17). Carelessness in moral behavior would be "unwise." Wise living involved "making the most of the time," literally "redeeming" or "buying up" the time. The word for time here is not the ordinary word for the passage of time but a word that denotes time as opportunity. The idea is that time that is not used wisely for Christian action is lost.

Timely action is especially important "because the days are evil." The fact that evil is widespread in the world at a certain time gives Christians all the more reason to live above that evil and to expose it. The latter half of the first century in the Roman Empire was a time of persecution and hardship for Christians, but it was also the time of greatest opportunity. Those who would neglect the challenge of Christian living in such a time of need were called "foolish." Those

who would be wise must "understand what the will of the Lord is."
The will of God is always the criterion and the motivation for Christian
living.

Verses 18-20 describe the quality of the Christian life in terms of
another contrast, the difference between the influence of alcohol and
the influence of the Spirit. From earliest human history, including
Bible times, people have turned to alcohol because of the temporary
feeling of well-being it gives them. The Bible consistently condemns
drunkenness, and Paul was saying here that the true well-being which
people are looking for comes when they are "filled with the Spirit."
The lift, energy, and good feelings people need are not provided
by chemicals but by the power of God working in their lives.

People frequently use alcohol when they are with other people
to make it easier to have a good time. But Paul described the gather-
ings of Christians as they are filled with the Spirit. They communicated
with each other with music. "Psalms" refer to the songs of Israel
found in the Old Testament and to similar Christian verses. "Hymns"
may have been new songs of the Christian faith, perhaps including
the verses quoted in 1:14. It is not clear how "spiritual songs" differ.
They may have been more spontaneous outbursts of praise.

While these songs are shared with one another, they are also expres-
sions of praise to God. They come from the hearts of the people.
They are accompanied by thanksgiving, which always had a special
significance for Paul. This thanksgiving was to be "always and for
everything," not just in favorable circumstances. Even when he was
suffering in prison, Paul expressed the song that was in his heart (Acts
16:25). This is possible only to those who know that God is their Father
through Jesus Christ.

Wives and Husbands (5:21-33)

Mutual submission (5:21).—The King James Version takes this
verse as the last phrase of the preceding discussion about spiritual
conduct. This is because "be subject" ("submitting" in the KJV) is a
participle, not an independent verb. The Revised Standard Version
and many modern commentators see this as one of several cases where
a participle is independent and serves an imperative verb. This is
also supported by the fact that there is no verb in the Greek after
"wives" in verse 22, so "be subject" must be understood as the verb
there.

Either way, this is a general word to all Christians to be subject or to submit to one another. The verb used is a military term meaning to line up under. This they are to do "out of reverence for Christ." "Reverence" here is literally "fear." This term is not usually used with reference to Christ, but it is frequently used of one's attitude to God, an attitude of respect and reverence. It is also appropriate to one's relationship with the Son of God.

This emphasis is a part of Paul's overall interest in the unity and harmony of the body of Christ. Each member of the body is to function in cooperation with others under Christ, who is the head (4:15-16). Such cooperation will often mean submission, putting one's own security, happiness, and well-being in second place to the security, happiness, and well-being of others. This is the example set by Jesus, who took the role of servant and washed his disciples' feet (Mark 10:43-45; John 13:3-16).

In the discussion that followed Paul showed how this principle applied to wives, husbands, children, parents, slaves, and masters. In each case it should be remembered that submission is not one-way and that all Christians are to be subject to each other and to Christ. These instructions show that the Christians in the early church had many questions about how their faith applied to their situation in life. The New Testament makes it clear that faith has a lot to do with every area of life.

Wives (5:22-24).—Since there is no verb expressed in this verse, it literally reads, "Wives, to your husbands, as to the Lord." The verb, "be subject," is supplied by verse 21. This makes it clear that the submission described is a part of the mutual submission that belongs to all Christians, and not the slavish obedience that ancient society prescribed for a wife. This submission is also a voluntary action of the wife, not something imposed upon her by her husband. The following verses (vv. 25-35) clearly show that the wife is not being asked to subject herself more than the husband is asked to subject himself. In fact, much more is said about the duties of the husband than of the wife in this chapter.

This passage is the center of much controversy today. Some feel that marriage should be an equal partnership with both sharing in the decision making on the same level. Others feel that there is an unchangeable division of roles that requires the husband to have the larger share of authority. This commentary cannot and should not attempt to resolve this larger issue. However, several observations can be made at this point. These words were written in a time when all the authority in the society belonged to men, and women had very few rights. Christ brought a new freedom and dignity to women, and Paul recognized that women and men are spiritual equals in Christ (Gal. 3:28). This passage does not approve the ancient customs regarding marriage and women any more than 6:5 approves the customs of slavery. Husbands and wives today must apply these teachings in Christian freedom with the guidance of the Holy Spirit, not in legalism and literalism.

The wife's submission to her husband is to be "as to the Lord." This is another sign that it is not the same as the obedience of wives to husbands in ancient pagan culture. All through this passage, Paul was thinking of the parallels between the family and the church. The husband's headship in the marriage is not that of a patriarch or authoritarian master. It is like the headship of Christ over the church—loving, self-giving, caring, and gentle. The wife's subjection—and the term subjection is hardly adequate to describe it—is like that of the church to Christ. It is trusting and confident that there is no harm to be feared in such a realtionship.

Husbands (5:25-33).—If Paul had in mind an authoritarian pattern of marriage, we might expect him at this point to urge husbands to exercise restraint in exerting their authority. But there is no mention of the husband's authority here. In chapter 6 parents and masters are urged not to provoke to anger or to threaten. But in chapter 5 the only counsel for husbands is to love. The Greek language has several words for love, and Paul could have used the word that means human, sensual love, from which we get our word *erotic.* Instead, he used the great Christian word that describes the kind of love God shows.

To illustrate this love he immediately turned to the greatest known example, the self-giving of Christ for his people. The parallel between the marriage of husband and wife on the one hand and the relation of Christ and the church on the other was uppermost in Paul's mind. It dominates the whole passage. The Old Testament often spoke of Israel as being married to God, and in Revelation the church is described as the bride of Christ. Here Paul emphasized the fact that Christ gave himself so the church would be holy, his own pure possession. He was both stating a truth about the church and setting forth an ideal for marriage. Christ is said to "sanctify the church having cleansed her by the washing of water with the word."

Several interpretations have been suggested for this phrase. Some think this is a reference to the bride's careful preparation for the wedding, including bathing. Some think the reference is to baptism, by which God's people are set apart and made members of the church. Others feel that the reference to water is simply a way of speaking of cleansing. It is significant that "the word" and not water itself is the agent of cleansing here.

In verses 28-29 the truth about Christ and the church is applied to marriage. The husband in loving his wife is actually loving his own body—that is, his own person or life. He can no more fail to love her than a man could hate himself and fail to care for himself. As Christ cherishes the church, the husband should cherish his wife. Christ does this because the church is his body. The husband does this because he and his wife, according to Genesis 2:24, are "one flesh."

The thought of the one-flesh union of marriage led Paul again to think of his great theme of the mystery revealed in Christ. This mystery is also about a union, the unity of all people in Christ and his body the church. The teaching of Genesis 2:24 applies to husbands and wives, but Paul also saw in it an application to Christ and the church.

Verse 33, beginning with "however," shows that Paul wanted to move back from his emphasis on the church to the immediate subject at hand, which was marriage. He repeated his plea that husbands should love their wives. Wives, in summary, were to respect their husbands. The word is literally "fear." This may reflect the accepted role of wives in the first century, but it is also influenced by Paul's conviction that Christians are to be subject to each other out of fear of, meaning reverence for, Christ (v. 21).

Children and Parents (6:1-4)

The counsel given to children was that they should obey their parents. There are two possible interpretations of the phrase "in the Lord." Some think that it means "as long as their requirements agree with the will of God." Thus it would have a special relevance to the Gentile world, where a child might have a parent who was not a believer. Others feel the phrase simply means "as a Christian should."

The added phrase, "for this is right," could also have several meanings. It may mean that the obedience of children is recognized as right by all people. Or it may reflect the fact that a child cannot always understand the reasons for a parent's instructions and must obey because it is the right thing to do.

Paul cited the fifth commandment at this point. It contains the broader word "honor." This means obedience in the case of younger children and respect and care in the case of older children. Paul called this the first commandment with promise, even though the second commandment indicates that God will show his love to those who keep his promises. This addition to the second commandment was not so much a promise as a statement about God made in connection with the description of God.

The fifth commandment has a more specific promise. Those who honor their parents will live long upon the earth. The original wording said, "in the land which the Lord your God gives you" (Ex. 20:12). The more general statement was used by Paul because it is more appropriate to Christians in that form. The promise means that a society that honors its elders will be a healthier, more stable society than the one that does otherwise.

There is a word for parents here, too. The word "fathers" is probably used in the general sense to include both parents. They are not to provoke their children to anger. Since they have authority over the child, it would be easy to be harsh. But parents are to recognize that children, too, have rights and feelings. Parental authority must be exercised with due regard for the child. They are to bring their children up in "discipline," a word which means positive instruction as well as correcting or chastening. "Instruction" is also needed. This is a more specific word for admonition or correction. The discipline and instruction of the Lord is what God can do in the children's life through faithful Christian parents.

Slaves and Masters (6:5-9)

In the Roman Empire of Paul's day, almost all work was done by slaves. A large portion of the population was in forced servitude either as captives of Roman conquest or as debtors who could not pay their obligations. Many of the early Christians were slaves like Onesimus, the servant of Philemon at Colossae. Paul wrote instructions similar to these for all the members of the household in his letter to the

Colossians. Here in Ephesians he again included slaves and masters in his words to the Christian family.

Looking back from an age which has finally abolished slavery, we may wonder why the early Christians did not oppose such an evil situation. But a little historical imagination tells us that the church was small and weak at that time and that slavery was strongly entrenched in the world. It probably did not occur to them that slavery could be eliminated. Such a change would require centuries of developing Christian conscience, and even then it would not be easy. A look at the abolition of slavery in America in the nineteenth century, or the effort to eliminate racial discrimination in the twentieth century, will help us not to judge the early Christians because they did not do more. On the contrary, it will make us take a closer look at the evils of our day to see what we should be doing now.

Paul's approach to the slavery problem was to urge masters and slaves to acknowledge Christ as their Lord. Slaves were to obey their earthly masters, literally "lords." They should accept the necessity of their situation and transform it into spiritual service to Christ, who was their heavenly Lord. They were to do this with "fear and trembling" because all Christian relationships were to be conducted in the fear of the Lord and because their earthly masters had great power over them. They were also to obey "in singleness of heart." Their service should be sincere and devoted, not just a superficial thing. They would be tempted to give "eye-service," the kind of work that only gave the best when the boss was looking.

Christians, however, were serving Christ even in their daily work. They were to work with constant goodwill, pleasing Christ as well as the boss. They were also to recognize that their work would be rewarded by the Lord. Good work was not always fully appreciated by the boss. It was not always adequately paid. But God would reward those who perform their earthly duties with Christian dedication. The words "whether he is a slave or free" remind us that these words are just as applicable to the modern employee as to the first-century slave.

Masters had a responsibility, too. They were to follow the same guidelines. They should avoid threatening. Circumstances had given them power over others, but this should not be used to manipulate or intimidate. Even the master had a master, the heavenly Lord. Even the boss was accountable to the higher power of God. In this respect, the servant and master were equal. In God's eyes, human status buys no extra privileges. The conviction that "there is no partiality with him" was very important to the early church in which so many were poor and oppressed. The word "partiality" literally means taking people at face value. Similar statements are made in Acts 10:34, Romans 2:11, Colossians 3:25, and 1 Peter 1:17.

The Whole Armor of God (6:10-20)

The fight against evil (6:10-13).—This passage, beginning with "finally," concludes the letter. It draws together a number of themes from throughout the book. In particular it looks back to 5:3-20, where evil deeds and evil days are described as enemies of God's people. Against this background, Paul counseled Christians to "be strong." More literally, he said, "be strengthened," for the strength needed was not their own but God's. The idea of being "in the Lord" was prominent throughout the book, for it was this union with Christ by faith that was the source of their new life and strength. "Be strengthened with might through his Spirit" was one of the blessings Paul prayed for them to have in 3:16. Now he urged them to receive what had been made available.

"The whole armor" which they were to put on is actually described by one word which has come over into English as "panoply." It is the total equipment of the soldier, both offensive and defensive. This is similar to putting on the new nature in 4:24. This equipment would enable them to stand against the enemy, who is the devil, already mentioned as a present danger in 4:27. His activity is described as "wiles" or clever and subtle tactics, mentioned in 4:14 as characteristic of cunning false teachers.

Paul stressed that the enemy was more than human. This was why the strength needed was divine strength. The enemy was described in terms similar to 1:21 and 3:10. Each of these is an enemy against which Christians contend, literally "wrestle." The list included "the principalities, . . . the powers, . . . the world rulers of this present darkness, . . . the spiritual hosts of wickedness in the heavenly places." This is a staggering lineup of spiritual forces and their human agents who war against God and his people. Many moderns are quick to dismiss such a vision of supernatural evil, but modern man has not been able to dismiss the power of evil so easily. This warning about the strength of the forces of evil needs to be taken seriously.

Because of this conflict with evil, Paul repeated his challenge to take the armor of God. The goal he had in mind was for God's people "to stand," repeated four times in this passage. Standing speaks of both stability and victory. It is the opposite of falling in battle.

Equipment for battle (6:14-17).—In this beautiful and graphic passage Paul pictured the Christian soldier being outfitted for battle. The image follows the picture of God arming himself with a breastplate of righteousness and a helmet of salvation in Isaiah 59:17. Thus the armor of God is both the armor he supplies and the armor he himself uses in the battle. The items of equipment are listed in the order they would be put on. Each is identified by the spiritual quality it represents; but since the emphasis is on the whole armor, the details of the individual pieces should not be pressed too far.

The first step in preparing for battle was to gird the loins. Men in ancient times wore long robes. These could hinder movement, so for work or battle they were pulled up and tied about the waist and hips with a girdle or belt. The belt in this case is truth, meaning sincerity and integrity of character. The idea of truth as the gospel is included in the later items of shoes and sword. The Christian who goes to fight against the lies of the devil must not be tripped up by any untruth in his own life.

The breastplate was vital, for it protected the heart and lungs. Righteousness does this for the Christian. His basic defense against evil is obedience to God's will and uprightness in his own conduct. Wrong attitudes and actions become weak spots in the armor through which the enemy thrusts his weapons.

Shoes were also important, as every foot soldier soon learns. Shoes that pinch, slip, or weigh down the step may make a crucial difference in the battle. For the Christian, it is the gospel of peace that makes his feet spring lightly across the field. Paul, like Isaiah, emphasized the feet of those who bring good news (Isa. 52:7; Rom. 10:15).

The shield specified here is the large shield for the whole body, about two and one-half by four feet in size. Made of leather and sometimes soaked in water, it could protect from the flaming arrows which burn as well as pierce. The Christian's shield is faith, the complete confidence he has in God's power. This willingness to let God's power work in our lives can counter all that the enemy throws at us. The "taking" described here is not grabbing with our own strength but receiving what is given.

The helmet protects the most vital and vulnerable part of all, the head. Salvation is the Christian's most basic protection. Because of

God's grace and the guarantee of eternal life, the soldier of Christ can be fearless. Nothing the enemy can do will break through the bond that holds him to God. There may be setbacks; but when the battle is over, his head will be held high.

The sword was the only offensive weapon included here, but the Christian is ready to attack as well as defend. His sword is the one provided by the Spirit. It is God's own weapon, the only one adequate for a spiritual battle, the Word of God. This refers to God's message whether spoken or written. Christ is the personal Word of God (John 1:1) and he himself wields the sword against the forces of evil (Rev. 19:15).

Preparation through prayer (6:18-20).—The first word of verse 18 is literally "praying," referring to the way all the previous things are to be done. This is the thought behind the hymn which says, "Put on the gospel armor,/Each piece put on with pray'r." [2] The military image drops into the background here, but prayer is the soldier's communication with headquarters. It is also the spirit with which the troops support one another. Modern armies call for air support. God's army calls for prayer support. This prayer is to be at all times, and the word here is the word for time as opportunity (see 5:16). Prayer is to be in the Spirit—that is, with the Sprit's help and with the Spirit as the medium of the Christian's life. It is to be prayer in general and supplication, or specific requests, in particular. The attitude of the prayer warrior is alertness and persistence. Like the guard posted before the camp, he is to be vigilant without letdown. His concern is to be for "all the saints." The individual soldier is not ready unless the whole army is ready.

In particular, Paul requested prayer for himself. His desire was for the ability to preach his message boldly. The phrase "opening my mouth" was one that is only used of very serious matters. Paul identified himself as "an ambassador in chains." This described his commitment to the gospel. There were many ambassadors in Rome at that time in fine embassies. Paul, though an ambassador of Christ, was in prison. He did not ask to be released, only to be empowered to speak.

Final Words (6:21-24)

Up to this point, Paul's personal words have been limited to identifying himself and explaining his mission to the Gentiles. Here at the end of the letter he acknowledged the personal ties between himself and some of his readers. The letter was to be sent by a personal messenger who would give them news of Paul and encourage them. He himself was a minister and a faithful one. The messenger was identified as Tychicus. These two verses are almost identical with Colossians 4:7-9, indicating that Tychicus carried both letters. In Colossians we learn that Onesimus the servant of Philemon was with Tychicus, so it is likely that Tychicus also delivered the letter to Philemon. Here we get a glimpse of one of the many lesser-known early Christians. Tychicus was associated with Paul at the end of his third missionary journey (Acts 20:4; 21:29). He is also mentioned in Titus 3:12 and 2 Timothy 4:12 as one who aided Paul in the last years of his ministry.

The book closes with a rich benediction. Now-familiar themes of peace, brotherhood, love, faith, and grace are the blessings Paul pronounced on God's people. He had spoken eloquently of Christ's love for his church. At the end he graced them with the title, "all who love our Lord Jesus Christ with love undying."

Note

1. Quoted in Francis Foulkes, *The Epistle of Paul to the Ephesians,* "The Tyndale New Testament Commentaries" (Grand Rapids: William B. Eerdmans Publishing Co., 1963), p. 133.
2. Words by George Duffield, Jr., 1858.

Bibliography

General

Allen, Clifton J., ed. *The Broadman Bible Commentary* 11. Nashville: Broadman Press, 1971.

Barclay, William. *The Letters to the Galatians and Ephesians.* Rev. ed. The Daily Study Bible Series. Philadelphia: The Westminster Press, 1976.

Hunter, Archibald M. *The Letter of Paul to the Galatians, The Letter of Paul to the Ephesians, et al.* The Layman's Bible Commentary. Richmond: John Knox Press, 1959.

2 Corinthians

Barclay, William. *The Letters to the Corinthians.* Rev. ed. The Daily Study Bible Series. Philadelphia: Westminster Press, 1975.

Foreman, Kenneth J. *Romans, 1 Corinthians, 2 Corinthians.* The Layman's Bible Commentary. Richmond: John Knox Press, 1961.

Tasker, R. V. G. *The Second Epistle of Paul to the Corinthians.* Tyndale Bible Commentaries, vol. 8. Grand Rapids: William B. Eerdmans Publishing Company, 1958.

Galatians

Allan, John A. *The Epistle of Paul the Apostle to the Galatians.* Torch Bible Commentaries. London: SCM Press, Ltd., 1951.

Cole, Robert Alan. *The Epistle of Paul to the Galatians.* The Tyndale New Testament Commentaries, vol. 9. Grand Rapids: William B. Eerdmans Publishing Company, 1965.

Tenney, Merrill C. *Galatians: The Charter of Christian Liberty.* Rev. ed. Grand Rapids: William B. Eerdmans Publishing Company, 1975.

Ephesians

Bruce, F. F. *The Epistle to the Ephesians.* Old Tappan, New Jersey: Fleming H. Revell Company, 1961.

Carver, W. O. *Ephesians: The Glory of God in the Christian Calling.* Nashville: Broadman Press, 1979.

Foulkes, Francis. *The Epistle of Paul to the Ephesians.* The Tyndale New Testament Commentaries, vol. 10. Grand Rapids: William Eerdmans Publishing Company, 1963.

Summers, Ray. *Ephesians: Pattern for Christian Living.* Nashville: Broadman Press, 1960.